Journey

Pathway to Freedom

Sharon Holburn

ISBN: 9781916787131

Contents

Acknowledgments

My first acknowledgment must go to my Jesus because He is the one who took my shattered and broken life and made it whole. He never left me; He was with me every step of the way. He is the one who healed me, the one who delivered me, and the one who set me completely and totally free. As I walked through the process, He held my hand in His to ensure that I would not falter or fall, after which He empowered and ordained me to do the same for others. In obedience to His will and His purpose for my life, I now have the privilege of setting the captives free in His wonderful and glorious name.

To my husband, Bob, my most valued and cherished friend. I will be forever grateful to God for bringing our lives together as one. Thank you for your encouragement, patience, your guidance, your love, and respect as I continue to grow into the woman of God that He has called me to be.

To a great man of God, Bud Ross, whose deliverance ministry was an integral part of my restoration.

To my friend, Beverley, for being a very special person in my life, being the sister that I never had.

About the Author

Sharon Holburn is a perfect example of how God can take an individual who was on a merry-go-round of neglect and abuse of all sorts and set her free to fulfill the plans He had for her life. Sharon is now a woman who is empowered to minister to other women who are where she once was. In doing so, she gives God the Glory for what He has done in her life, having taken her from being a survivor to being an overcomer.

Endorsement

Truly the Lord has given Sharon Holburn beauty for ashes, the oil of joy for mourning, and a garment of praise for the spirit of heaviness, that she might be called an oak of righteousness, a planting of the Lord, that He might be glorified.

Sharon's **JOURNEY** is an account of one woman whose life destiny appeared to be a merry-go-round of bondage, victimization, rejection, loneliness, and deep emotional pain –

BUT GOD – literally brought her into life, love, wholeness, and purpose. This is a **real** testimony, without apology, shame, or religiosity. She boldly declares things as they were and as they now are. Her story will bring hope to the many who feel there's no way "out" as they come to meet their champion, Jesus.

Mary Audrey Raycroft - founder of Releasers of Life.

Introduction

The first time I met Sharon was in early February of 1995 when I was part of Ajax Christian Community Fellowship, a small evangelical church in southern Ontario, Canada. She had arrived at the church in the company of her friend, Josie, having finally accepted an invitation from Josie to attend a Sunday evening service.

Being a small church, it was easy to pick out any new faces, so when they walked into the sanctuary that evening, I could tell immediately that she was a visitor. It was obvious by her posture that she was feeling a little self-conscious and awkward, no doubt due to being in the midst of this group of strangers. She dropped her head a little and hurriedly made her way to a row of seats in front of where I was sitting, where she sat down.

To welcome her and to help put her at ease, I leaned forward and said, "Hello." When I got over the fact that she totally ignored me, I remember thinking to myself that she had obviously suffered some serious damage and that she had come to the right place to be healed of it.

At that moment in time, I had absolutely no idea of how God was going to move in her life and how the move that He made was going to affect mine. If anyone had ever suggested to me that five years down the road, Sharon and I would be husband and wife, I probably would have laughed and responded, "You must be joking!"

Over the next few years, I became aware of the many circumstances that Sharon was dealing with. I learned that her life experiences were, to say the least, extreme and that the resulting stress levels were seriously affecting her health. Her defense mechanisms were running on overdrive, having been finely tuned to the point where she demonstrated attitude in everything she said and did. Like so many hurt and broken people, she had a cold, hardened, distant look about her, having built walls upon walls around her broken heart in an effort to protect herself. As you read about her Journey, about her Pathway to Freedom, you will to some degree, relive the experiences that she has lived through. In doing so, I believe that you will come to a better appreciation and understanding of why she was the way she was. But more importantly, I believe you will come to appreciate and understand that with Jesus, there is hope.

In my lifetime, I have met many people who have lived through difficult times, yet none can come close to what Sharon has lived through. Over a period of 35 years, she was badly neglected as a child and suffered many kinds of abuse -

physical, sexual, emotional, and psychological, to name a few. She was preyed upon and sexually abused by her mother's boyfriend, a man who was thirty-three years her senior. For twenty years, she lived in a relationship with this man who manipulated her on a continual basis while using her for his own gratification. Yet, in helping to document her Journey, I have come to a greater understanding of how God is always active in our lives, even when the circumstances we are living through are at their worst. Regrettably, some who read this book will see Sharon as nothing more than a survivor. The truth is this, Sharon is much more than a survivor; in every sense of the word, she is an overcomer.

Sharon's Journey has now brought her to the place where she has dealt with all her past hurts and the resulting brokenness. The walls that she erected to protect her broken heart, the walls that took years to build up, are now a pile of rubble at the feet of Jesus. The attitude and the hardness are gone, and what is left is a flawless jewel. Like a precious stone, the woman I married has many facets. While she is fragile, delicate, loving, sensitive, and compassionate, she is also strong and confident, now knowing who she is in Christ.

When Sharon first mentioned to me that she felt led to write about her Journey, my immediate response was, "Do it!" As I have worked with her to put this book together, I have learned so much more about her, much of which is not contained within these covers. In writing about her Journey, Sharon has made herself transparent to all. By disclosing many of her inmost secrets, she has exposed the very essence of her being to all who will read this book. You might be asking yourself, "Why would anyone want to do that?" The answer is simple. Sharon's desire is to see people set free, and by sharing her Journey, she believes that it will encourage and uplift those who, at this time, are where she once was.

Pastor Bob Holburn

1

My Early Years

My journey began on Halloween night on the 31st of October 1963. The weather outside was seasonably cool, as it usually was at that time of the year in southern Ontario. Inside, the little people were "Trick or Treating," going from door to door down the hallway of the apartment building where Verne and Ron Sills were living. A pregnant Verne was patiently waiting for the birth of their first child, who really wasn't in any hurry to make an appearance. The baby was overdue, and the air was filled with expectations of the big event and when it would happen. While they were patiently waiting, Verne and Ron were passing the time playing poker with Skinny and Muriel, Ron's brother and sister-in-law.

The story, as it has been told many times, goes like this; Verne found herself holding a royal flush, and at the very moment she stood up to lay it down and claim her winnings, her water broke. It had finally happened, the big event was on, so she immediately dropped her winning hand and made the announcement, "Ron, it's time." As Ron hurriedly steered Verne and her suitcase down the hallway to the elevator, Verne was busy pulling her curlers out of her hair and stuffing them into her handbag. The time in the elevator was well used to brush out her hair and apply some makeup; after all, she had to look her best as she was giving birth to their first baby. Following a hair-raising drive to the hospital at Weston, Ontario, Verne was admitted and was quickly moved into the maternity ward. After a short period of labor, I finally arrived on the scene making my debut at 11:58 pm, Sharon Anne Sills, weighing in at a mere 6 lbs. 3 ozs. When the nurse announced my arrival to my father, telling him that he had a daughter, he was quite disappointed. When he was finally allowed in to see my mother, his first words to her were, "I didn't want a girl". So it was that the seeds of rejection were sown into my life, spoken into existence by my very own father, a man who wanted a son and not a daughter.

From what I have learned from my mother, the next 18 months were very good for all three of us. There was a measure of peace and stability in the home, and my father had accepted the fact that he had a daughter, not that he had much choice in the matter anyway. Now that he had a family to support, my father had been looking around for a better job, one that would provide him with an immediate increase in income as well as an excellent long-term opportunity. He found exactly what he was looking for when he was offered a job in commercial refrigeration and sales, with a company that was located in London, Ontario. By taking on this new job, the family had no choice but to relocate, and so it was that we all moved to

Komoka, a small town just outside of London. My mother also went back to work as an occupational therapist, being fortunate enough to find employment in a local nursing home. Since my father's occupation required him to work very long and somewhat irregular hours, he was often gone from early in the morning and did not return home till the early hours of the next morning. His extended absence from the home and from the marriage put a terrible strain on the family and this subsequently contributed greatly to my mother falling into depression. Over a period of time, my mother became increasingly dependent on prescription drugs and alcohol to help her through the day. As she slipped down into that pit of addiction, she became more and more incapable of attending to my needs and became totally intolerant of any interference with her drinking. The situation got so bad that my very life was in jeopardy. She was a time bomb waiting to go off, and it was just a matter of time before she did me some physical harm.

The situation came to a head during one of my mother's drinking bouts, which just happened to coincide with me cutting some of my back teeth. I had been upset and crying for hours due to the pain, and she had been unable to relieve it or settle me down. Having reached the point where she couldn't take any more of my crying, in a drunken stupor, she managed to dial the right number and was able to get my father on the phone. She told him that she had had enough and that if he did not come home immediately, she was going to kill me. I thank God that my father responded as quickly as he did by coming straight home because when he rushed through my bedroom door, he found my mother standing over my crib with a knife in her hand. When my mother sobered up, my father impressed upon her the seriousness of this incident, and this led to her going for psychiatric help. After several consultations, her psychiatrist's diagnosis was that she was afraid of being isolated, afraid of being alone. My mother shared with me in later years that the root cause of her fear was the fact that when she was a child, her grandmother frequently locked her in a dark closet. She had been severely damaged by the actions of a mean and nasty old woman who did not like her or want her around, actions which had opened the door to a spirit of fear. This generational curse that was passed down from her grandmother would even affect me in my life up until a few weeks before my mother's death.

As is all too often the case, the psychiatrist who was treating my mother was limited to prescribing sleeping pills and tranquilizers, which only helped her to cope with her fears. He wasn't equipped or able to provide her with the inner healing that she required; subsequently, he could only deal with the symptoms and the resulting manifestation of fear. Had my mother followed the directions given and kept alcohol out of the equation, the prescription drugs may have had an impact on her. Unfortunately, prescription drugs and alcohol do not mix well and the fighting between my mother and father escalated to the point where it was virtually constant. One night, when I was about four years old, I was rudely awakened by the noise of their fighting, and I climbed out of bed to see what all the noise was about. With my dolly in one hand, I remember opening my bedroom door with the other and slowly making my way to the top of the stairs. The closer I got to the top of the stairs, the louder the screaming and yelling became, and I was almost afraid to take the last few steps. I stopped for a moment, took a deep breath, and two steps later arrived at the top of the stairs. When I looked down the stairs, I saw what all the noise was about. My petite 5' tall mother was straddling my 6' 2" tall father, who was on his back on the floor. She had him at quite a disadvantage and was in the process of strangling him with his own tie, which was obviously causing him some distress. When they both realized that they had an audience at the top of the stairs, the encounter was broken off and I was encouraged by both of them to get back to bed with my dolly.

The situation between my mother and father continued to deteriorate, and it was just a matter of time until they separated, with my mother and me staying in Komoka and my father moving to London. Even though I hadn't seen my father very much due to his work schedule, he had now disappeared from my life completely. To a little 4-year-old girl, it seemed that one minute he was there and the next he was not, and I used to wonder where my daddy had gone and what it was that I had done to make my daddy go away. With my father now completely out of the picture, the fighting and arguing had come to a complete stop. Let's face it; it was difficult for my mother to fight with herself. Although the fighting had stopped, her drinking problem only got worse, and as she consumed more and more alcohol, she became the sole focus of her life. This process caused her to become totally oblivious to my needs, and since she was incapable of caring for me, she continually left me alone to take care of myself. I very quickly became a self-sufficient four-year-old. Even when I came home from the hospital after having my tonsils removed, I had to get my own cold drinks to soothe my throat because my mother was too drunk to do anything for me. More and more I felt abandoned. I was lost and alone, my daddy had left me behind and my mother didn't care.

Now that my mother and I were living alone in the country, she decided that we required some additional protection. Her solution to dealing with all of her fear was to purchase Rocky, a large purebred German shepherd. Rocky had been trained as a police dog, and he had obviously been trained very well as he quickly became my protector. He never strayed very far from my side, and anyone who got too close to me saw how nice and white and sharp his teeth were. Unfortunately, after only having him for a couple of months, Rocky wrongly perceived the paper delivery boy as a threat to me, and he attacked him in our driveway. Fortunately, the paper delivery boy was just badly shaken up and was not seriously injured. After this incident, my mother thought that it was best to get rid of Rocky as she couldn't take the risk of him going after some other poor innocent. It wasn't long after his departure that my mother and I also had to move since my mother was spending most of her money on alcohol and was having trouble paying the rent. I am sure that my mother thought that the move was a good idea as she could then rent a smaller house or an apartment, freeing up some more cash for her to spend on booze.

I can still remember that I didn't want to move away from Komoka. I guess I probably thought that if we moved away and my father came looking for me, he wouldn't be able to find me. In spite of what I thought or felt, the move happened anyway, and my mother and I moved to London, where she had rented a small house. The move was a traumatic experience for me, and the effects were compounded when my mother informed me that my father was divorcing her. I was so devastated by this news that, to this day, I have no memory of what happened during that time. Even my memory of the subsequent months is non-existent, having been mentally blocked out. My mother later told me that I had taken the divorce so badly that she was unable to go to work for almost six months. When I eventually began to show signs of recovery, my mother was able to go back to work, taking on two jobs, so that she would be able to buy the small house that we were living in.

Shortly after coming through the trauma of my mother and father getting divorced, I was old enough to attend public school. To the best of my recollection, my time spent in grades one and two was fairly normal, that is, normal by my standards. I was still affected to some degree by the absence of my father, particularly since I didn't know where he was, and I truly felt that something important was missing from my life. My mother continued to be angry and miserable all the time, and this just seemed to fuel her need to drink more and more. By the time I was in grade three, I was already beginning to show all the signs of neglect. Because of her drinking, my mother had absolutely no interest in me at all. I was just someone who was always there, someone who was not a priority or of any consequence. It became increasingly evident that she had no concern for my dress, my appearance, my health, or my general welfare.

At school, it was becoming more and more obvious to the other kids that I was just not like them, particularly since I didn't have pretty clothes and shoes to wear. Because of my lack, I was labeled as the poor kid and soon became the person that everybody felt they had a right to pick on. One day some boys in the schoolyard thought that they would have some fun at my expense. Three or four of them grabbed hold of me and put a huge green grass snake down the back of my shirt. The fear and terror of that incident are still with me to this day, and the result of that experience is that I am terrified of snakes. Even to this day, I have great difficulty just looking at one. Another time some boys grabbed me, wrapped a heavy rope around my neck, and then began to play tug of war with my neck in the middle. I was completely helpless, unable to free myself and stop myself from being choked. With my air supply cut off, I was unable to breathe and, therefore, unable to cry out for help. Even if I had been able to cry out in the hope of getting somebody's attention, my cry would probably have been drowned out by the laughter of those participating in the game. When they had finished with me, I had a rope burn all the way around my neck. I can still remember the excruciating pain. When my mother found out what had happened at school, she did absolutely nothing about it, and as painful as my rope burn was, my mother's lack of response hurt me more.

I really don't know how to explain how I felt at that time, other than to say that my life seemed to be absolutely hopeless. I was totally alone with no one to listen to me, no one to help me, and definitely no one to rescue me. I was just a little kid out there on my own, abandoned by my father, ignored by my mother, and tormented by all of the kids at school. I just did not understand why the other kids were picking on me, why they were being so mean to me, and it didn't take long before I began to dread going to school. My mother was totally oblivious to what was happening to me, and any hope I had of this change was lost as her drinking was getting worse by the day. As her nightlife was picking up, she would often drop me off at a sitter's house while she and her friend Gloria would go to the bar for the evening. She would get so drunk that she would forget where she had left me and would have to do the rounds of all the different sitters that she used until she found me. There were times when my mother was short of cash, and paying a sitter wasn't in her budget. When that was the case, I was left home alone and would usually spend the time in my bedroom closet, playing with my doll and my budgie. On the night that my budgie died, even though my mother arrived home drunk as usual, she was still able to tell me to put him in a shoebox and bury him in the backyard. She did not console me in any way. She didn't see the loss on my face and she certainly didn't realize that I had lost my best friend. He was my little buddy who had kept me company when she wasn't home. He was the one that I shared all my secrets with, all of my hopes and dreams, and now he was gone.

As a child of seven or eight, I would often arrive home from school to find an empty house because at that time my mother was working two jobs. I was left to fend for myself until she arrived home from work, which usually was between ten and eleven at night. When I arrived home from school, I would play for a while until I got hungry. I would then make myself some supper and eat it while I was watching television. It was a very lonely time for me and the sense of abandonment that I felt then followed me into adulthood. One day, after coming home from school, I was reaching for a cup so that I could get a drink. Since I couldn't reach the cups in the cupboard, I had to jump up onto the counter and, in the process of doing this, I hit my head on the corner of the open cabinet door. Needless to say, I literally saw stars! Even though my head hurt so much, I thought I was okay until I saw the blood trickling down the front of my glasses. I had cut my head open on the corner of the cabinet door, and, as usual, there was no one there to help me, but me. On the weekends, when I was left home alone, I would often go to the end of the street and play in the forest where there was a huge fallen oak tree that I used to sit on. I would sit up there and wish that I had somebody to play with, but there was no one. Sometimes I would even talk to God, telling him all my secrets and how I felt about things. Sometimes I would just sit on the front porch of our house and watch the other kids playing, hoping that they would see me and let me play with them, but they didn't how I hated being different! How I hated being alone!

How I hated being me!

2

Dad Under The Gun

Shortly after we moved from Komoka to London, my mother was persuaded by some of her drinking buddies to track down my father. The motivation behind this action was to see if she could get child support from him, which would obviously supplement her drinking money. I am not sure if she personally managed to track him down or if she had someone else do it for her. All I know is that one day she got a phone call, and the party on the other end of the line gave her the address where my father was living. It turned out that my father was living in a house that was only two blocks away from us. Apparently, my father had been residing there for some time with his new girlfriend Mary-Lou, and her two children. Now that she had the information she required, my mother had a couple of drinks before calling for a cab. She then told me to get ready to go as soon as the cab arrived, and she even managed to squeeze in another drink while we were waiting.

Finally, the cab arrived and pulled into our driveway. We both got into the cab, and my mother gave the driver the address she had been given over the phone. After a short drive, we arrived at a small, detached home where we could see my father's truck parked in the driveway. My mother got out of the cab and told the cab driver to wait for her, and after telling me to stay in the cab, she walked over to my father's truck. She checked to see if the driver's door was locked and, finding it open, she pulled the driver's seat forward, exposing my father's shotgun which he always kept stored behind his seat. She removed the shotgun and cradled it on her left arm. She casually walked up to the front door of the house, knocked, and waited patiently to see who would open it. I don't know if the shotgun was loaded or not. I can only assume that my mother figured that having the shotgun in her hand would guarantee her getting my father's undivided attention.

After a minute or so, a little girl answered the front door, and although I could not hear what was said, I could see that she was speaking with my mother. I later learned that my mother asked her if her mommy or her mommy's boyfriend were home as she really needed to speak to either of them. The little girl said that they were both very busy and that they couldn't come to the door at that time. My mother then suggested to her that since they couldn't come to the door, maybe she could take her to where they were. The little girl agreed, and after taking my mother by the hand, she led her into the house and down the hallway, where she stopped right in front of the bathroom door. When my mother opened the door, she found my father and Mary-Lou taking a bath together. I can only imagine what went through their minds when they realized that there was a little woman with a shotgun standing at their bathroom door. There was no avenue of escape for them, for the doorway was blocked, and the bathroom window was a little too small to climb out of, and either way, they were both naked. My mother pointed the shotgun at my father and ordered him out of the tub. Then she marched him naked and dripping down the hallway into the bedroom. My mother told me that when she spoke with my father in the bedroom, the conversation focused primarily on the subject of child support and the need for me to visit with my father. After the negotiations were completed, my mother left the house and returned my father's shotgun to his truck. She got back into the cab, and we returned home, where she proceeded to have a few more drinks to celebrate a very successful operation.

Now that I knew for sure that my father was alive and well, I began to have some expectations, and I truly believed that my life was going to change for the better. After being under the gun, my father began to send me the occasional gift, which was usually an item of clothing for me to wear. He had obviously realized that my mother's need for alcohol was consuming all her finances and that clothing and footwear for me were not her priority. I remember, on one occasion, getting a new pair of shoes from him, and I was so excited to try them out on the front porch. As I skipped up and down the porch, I deliberately made a lot of noise so that my friend, Ella, who lived across the street, would notice me and ask me what I was doing. I wanted so badly to be able to tell her that my father had bought me a new pair of shoes and I was quite disappointed when she ignored me and didn't say anything. I guess I shouldn't have been surprised at this as Ella would often dump me as soon as someone else came along, someone whom she viewed as better off. As time passed, my father began to regularly pick me up on Friday afternoons and take me for the whole weekend. He would often take me camping at the provincial park along with Mary-Lou and her two kids, Randy and Rona-Lind. As my relationship with my father began to be restored, I found myself looking more and more to him as the person who would rescue me from my mother. Since my mother's focus continued to be on herself, it was only natural for me to expect that my father would not only fill the void but would possibly even replace her.

Then came the night of the big storm, with torrential rain and thunder and lightning. It was spectacular, it was bright, it was loud, and it was really scary. It was also very late, and my mother had not yet come home, with the lightning causing all kinds of strange shadows on the walls. My imagination was running wild, and I was scared out of my wits. Unable to reach my mother, I thought that it would be okay for me to call my father for help. So, I picked up the phone and called him, telling him that I was home alone and that I didn't know where my mother was and that I was really frightened by the storm. My father came over right away and picked me up, taking me back to Mary-Lou's house where, after a drink of milk, I was tucked into the top bunk of a set of bunk beds. When my mother finally arrived home to find a note telling her I was with my father, she was absolutely furious that I had called him. She immediately took a cab over to Mary-Lou's house, where she stormed in and hauled me out of the top bunk by my hair, after which she dragged me out to the cab half asleep. I paid dearly for this episode, for what she called embarrassing her in front of my father and his girlfriend. On the one hand, my mother felt embarrassed that my father and his girlfriend now knew that she wasn't there for me, while on the other hand, it was okay for her to do what she was doing as long as no one else knew. Even to this day, I have great difficulty understanding this aspect of neglect, where the perpetrator is okay with what is happening as long as nobody else knows about it.

Now that I was spending more and more time with my father, I began to see that his drinking problem was getting just as bad as my mother's. When I would spend the weekend with my father and Mary-Lou, it seemed to me that all they did was sit around and drink. Pretty soon, my visits with my father became nothing more than a change of location. It was the same story, just in a different place. During my fourth or fifth time at the cottage with them, things really took a turn for the worse, and I really got to see my father as I had never seen him before. All of us kids, Randy, Rona-Lind, and I, had all been up very late the previous night, and it just so happened that I was the last one to get out of bed that morning. My father was in an extremely bad mood and was absolutely miserable due to the fact that he was nursing a major hangover. On top of his discomfort, he was upset at me because I was the last to get out of bed and had missed breakfast. To ensure that I would not get any breakfast, he barked out an order to Rona-Lind, telling her to take the breakfast leftovers out and feed them to the dog. Rona-Lind called to me and said, "Sharon, why don't you come and help me?" As we were making our way out the screen door, Rona-Lind said, "Here, Sharon, do you want some? You didn't get any breakfast." As I reached out to take a piece of bacon from the plate she was holding, my father jumped off the chair he was sitting on and flew out through the screen door like a wild man. As he came through the door, he grabbed me with one hand and threw me over his knee while with his other hand, he grabbed the closest thing, which just so happened to be a piece of 2 x 4 lumber. In one continuous motion, he laid that piece of lumber full force across my backside. In excruciating pain and in absolute terror of my own father, I peed my pants, and, in the process, I peed all over his lap. I was so overwhelmed by fear and so brokenhearted at what my father had done to me that I couldn't even think straight. I was emotionally devastated that this man, whom I thought was going to be my savior, could do what he had done to me.

Determined not to get into any more trouble, I kept a low profile and stayed out of everyone's way, particularly my father's. Later that same day, my father came out and started up his truck, and announced to everyone that he was taking us down to the beach so that we could all go swimming. He yelled out specific orders to all of us kids, followed by the directive that we were to get into the truck immediately. Only too happy to comply, all of us kids piled into the front seat of my father's truck, where I took my usual place, sitting right next to my father. While we were waiting for my father and Mary-Lou to get the towels and whatever else they were bringing, Randy, Mary-Lou's son, deliberately pushed his foot forward and hit the gas pedal. It seemed as if my father appeared out of nowhere, and in a split second, the truck door flew open, and he jumped into the cab. In one fluid motion, he backhanded me across the face, and once again, I was emotionally devastated by what he had done. Without asking who was responsible or how it had happened, he assumed that I was the guilty party because I was closest to the pedal. I never had the opportunity to say that I was innocent; he chose to be judge, jury, and executioner. Through my tears, I said to him, "Daddy,

I didn't do it, Randy did it." His response was to tell me to "Shut up," and that is exactly what I did. I didn't speak to him for the rest of the day. When we finally returned to London that night, my father and Mary-Lou started drinking again, and I remember just sitting alone in the bedroom wondering why he hated me so much, hoping and praying that somebody would just take me home. As the evening wore on, my father eventually called a cab and sent me home in it. Just as well, for neither he nor Mary-Lou was fit to drive. On arriving home, I ran into my mother's arms and cried. I sobbed out my story, telling her every little detail of what had happened, and finished by telling her that I didn't want to see my father again. I had no idea at the time that I would be fourteen years old before I would see or speak to my father again.

Now that my father was no longer in the picture, my mother threw me for a loop by completely changing her M.O. She went from leaving me home all the time to taking me with her everywhere she went, not that we went to a lot of different places. While making the rounds of the bars, my mother met and became friends with Gloria, a woman very much like my mother, a woman who also had a drinking problem. Gloria became my mother's drinking buddy, and they got together every opportunity they could, which was basically every night. After supper, we would make our way over to Gloria's house, where she and my mother would drink themselves into oblivion. I would do my homework, read a book, watch television, or sometimes just sit there and watch them drink. I would sit there wishing that they would hurry up and get drunk so that I could go home. Once they began drinking, they lost all concept of time, and even though I had school the next day, we often didn't leave Gloria's house until one or two in the morning. It wasn't very long before they decided to put me to good use, and so it was that I was trained and promoted to the position of bartender. Mixing drinks for them was easy for me and convenient for them, as the less time they spent mixing, the more time they could spend drinking. I soon realized that if I mixed them a double, they didn't say anything, so after they had consumed three or four single drinks, I would start to mix them doubles. My plan actually worked quite well, after all. The sooner they got drunk, the sooner I got to go home to bed.

One memorable night, in spite of being extremely drunk, my mother decided that she and I were going to have a race to see who would get home first. Due to her condition at the time, she was far from steady on her feet, but I certainly wasn't going to be the one to tell her. And so, after a three, two, one, go, the race began with the two of us running as fast as we could down the sidewalk. As her speed increased, her stability decreased, and while making a right-hand turn to cross over the main road, it happened. My mother failed to negotiate the drop from the curb to the road level, her ankle twisted, and her leg folded beneath her, causing her to do a face plant on the road. On impact, her purse burst open, and all the contents spilled out, scattering everything she had in her purse all over the road. Fortunately, it was after one in the morning, and there was little or no traffic on the road at that time. As she slowly picked herself up, it was obvious that she was in considerable pain. In spite of her intoxicated condition, my mother's first instincts were to recover all her belongings which were now strewn all over the road. She was also extremely anxious that no one should see her crawling about on the road picking up her things, so she asked me to help her. After we had picked up everything, we slowly crossed the street, and as she limped and staggered the rest of the way home, I had to remain a few steps behind her with my hand over my mouth to muffle my laughter.

The next morning when my mother got up to go to work, she was nursing a very swollen ankle, not realizing at that time that she had actually cracked a bone in her ankle. Over the course of the day, the pain in her ankle diminished, and she assumed that she was just dealing with a badly sprained ankle. When she arrived home from work that evening, she hurriedly cooked and ate her supper and then got ready to go out to the bar with the girls, once again leaving me home alone. Let's face it, having a badly sprained ankle wasn't going to stop her from going out drinking with the girls. However, she did live to regret her decision as later that night, when she and the girls were leaving the bar, she stumbled and fell out the door. This time she really did some serious damage to herself as the impact of her fall completely broke the cracked bone in her ankle. The next morning when I saw my mother, you can imagine how shocked I was to see that she now had a cast on her leg. For the first time, my mother was totally immobilized, not able to go to work, not able to go to Gloria's house, and not able to do the rounds of the bars. Now that she was unable to go out drinking every night with her friends, she was reduced to drinking alone at home, and this caused her to become extremely depressed. Her friends, whom she would normally drink with, were noticeably absent during this forcible confinement, and after the removal of her cast, my mother continued to do her drinking alone at home.

As unpredictable as my mother was, what she did next surpassed her previous exploits. Without telling me anything about her plans, my mother sold our house and called in an auctioneer to remove and sell off all our furniture. I only found out what was happening when one afternoon, a large truck showed up in our driveway, and a number of men got out of the cab. There was a knock at the door, and my mother, who was half in the bag as usual, casually answered the door wearing nothing but a short pink nighty! You cannot begin to imagine what went through my mind when I realized that these people were here to remove all our furniture. My mother told me to sit down on the floor and stay out of the way while the auctioneer and his people did what they had come to do. They removed absolutely everything from that house that wasn't nailed down, except for my mother's box spring and mattress and her television. They even took my bed, not that it mattered much anyway, as I was rarely allowed to sleep in it. But it was mine, and when you do not have much, what you do have is important to you.

Although at the time it seemed like forever, for almost two months, we lived in that house with only a box spring and mattress and one television. During that time, all my mother did was lounge on her bed with her bottle of rye whisky in one hand and her other hand in a bowl of popcorn. When the day finally came that we were to move out of the house, she decided that it was time to tell me that she had purchased a fully furnished triplex on the other side of town. After keeping me in suspense for months, my mother finally explained to me her reason for moving. She explained to me that the rental income from the apartments in the triplex would cover the mortgage, allowing us to live rent-free. In retrospect, her living mortgage-free meant that she had just freed up more money to spend on booze. Having access to additional free income did not change my lot in life, as none of it was ever spent on me to meet my needs. Life continued for me as it always was. The only thing that changed was the geographical location.

3

Gabe And His Boys

Now that we had moved into the basement apartment of the triplex she had purchased, my mother was quite delighted that her plan appeared to be coming together. The basement apartment itself was very small, consisting of three small rooms, a tiny kitchen, and a small bathroom with a door so narrow that you had to go through it sideways. Above us were three medium-sized apartments, all of which had been rented out prior to us moving in, so from the very beginning, all of them were generating income for my mother. It wasn't too long before she discovered that all was not as it seemed and that being a landlord wasn't everything that she had expected it to be. She was approached by one of her tenants, who informed her that the tenant on the top floor had two outside cats, both of whom were heavily infested with fleas. This news was of great concern to my mother due to the fact that she was extremely allergic to fleabites. There was something in her blood that attracted fleas. She was like a flea magnet, and if there were only one flea in the house, it would pass me by and head for her. The magnitude of the flea infestation would only become apparent when one morning she woke up completely covered in blood, the result of literally hundreds of fleabites.

Her first response was to scream in fear, which quickly turned into anger towards the fleas, the cats, and their owner, in that order. Having an allergic reaction to the fleabites, she was rushed to the nearby hospital for treatment, where the hospital medical staff estimated that she had over two thousand fleabites on her body. It's hard to imagine that she could get that many fleabites in such a short period of time, but she did. She was absolutely covered in little red dots. After being treated and released from the hospital, my mother immediately headed back home, where she had the cats removed and called in a pest control company to fumigate the whole triplex. She was so stressed over these events that the doctor at the hospital gave her a prescription for nerve pills which, when taken along with her daily diet of alcohol, only added fuel to the fire.

After the big flea fiasco, life took a phenomenal change for us as we entered into a period of calm and tranquility where things settled down considerably for my mother. After years of upset and chaos, life actually became quite humdrum for her, to the point that she was always nervous and uneasy, probably wondering when the roof was going to fall in. She was experiencing a measure of peace and stability that had not been present in her life for years, not since shortly after I was born. This newfound peace and stability brought her a new measure of confidence in herself, which in turn brought about in her the desire to get back into the dating game. She was still going out to the bars at night, and I was still coming home from school to an empty house where I continued to take care of all my own needs. Shortly after my tenth birthday, my mother met and started to date a man called Gabe. Gabe was a divorcee who owned his own home in London, where he lived with his two young boys. Initially, my mother would meet Gabe at the bar, where they would spend the evening together. Since Gabe had two young boys at home, he usually didn't stay out too late, and this was a good thing because he would drop my mother off at home at a reasonable hour. As things between my mother and Gabe began to get serious, their relationship began to have a major effect on what little time I did spend with my mother. When my mother would arrive home from work, she would only stay home long enough to put together the makings of a meal for Gabe and his boys. She never included me; she always left me home alone while she took a cab to Gabe's house, where she would cook supper for him and his two boys. She never cooked me my supper before she left. She never asked me how my day had gone. She never asked me what I was going to do while she was out. It was like I didn't exist.

After a couple of months of this, my mother announced to me that she had sold the triplex and that we were both moving in with Gabe and his boys. I wasn't too happy about making a move into Gabe's house, particularly since it meant that, once again, I would have to change schools, and I didn't want to change schools. I was now in grade four, obviously older than I had been during my previous moves, and I had now formed some attachments with my teachers. I felt that this move was going to destroy my world, but when I voiced my concerns to my mother, they fell on deaf ears. She wasn't interested at all in hearing what I had to say. She was only focused on what she felt she needed at that time. I'm not sure if my mother took into consideration that Gabe's house was on the other side of town and that transportation to her place of employment was going to be an issue. She didn't drive or own a car. She was totally dependent on public transportation, and there was none from Gabe's house to where she worked. When the realization of this finally hit home, she had to quit her job and look for a new one closer to Gabe's home. Although it didn't take her long to find a new job, the one that she found required her to work rotating shifts, which was going to have a greater effect on me than on her. Even though my mother was with Gabe, she was still drinking heavily and still using prescription drugs. In spite of having someone in her life, it was business as usual as she continued on her downhill slide. As for me, the biggest difference I was dealing with was the fact that I wasn't left home alone. At last, I had some other kids to play with. Little did I know that Gabe was planning to take advantage of this situation and that my being left in his care would begin the nightmare of sexual abuse that would follow me into adulthood.

It all started so innocently with Gabe coming into the bathroom while I was having a bath just to check up on me, just to see if I was okay. One thing led to another, and as Gabe's plan unfolded, he began to make excuses that enabled him to send his boys to bed early. When he did this, he always had an excuse or a reason that would allow me to stay up and watch television with him. He would lie down beside me on the floor, where he would very casually lift up my nightgown and rub my bare bottom, caressing and fondling me. Gabe was quite creative in looking for ways to get his hands on me, and he would often use his boys to set up a situation where he could do so without it being too obvious. When I would use the washroom on the main floor, Gabe would get his boys, and they would be waiting for me when I came out. As I started to make a run for the stairs to get to my bedroom, the three of them would chase me, overwhelm me and throw me to the floor. Gabe would then have his boys hold me down while he pulled off my leotards and underwear, fully exposing me to all. It was all presented to his boys as good fun, and he would always put on a big show for them, pretending to play around so that they would not realize what he actually had in mind. The boys enjoyed this whole process very much as they thought it was great fun that their dad was helping them pick on a girl. Now that I was down on the floor, Gabe would send the boys away, and with me kicking and screaming, he continued to hold me down so he could fondle me. Like so many victims of this type of abuse, I was totally helpless, outnumbered, and terrified to speak to anyone about it, especially my mother.

In spite of the abuse that was going on, there were times when Gabe's boys and I really got along quite well together. This was probably due to the fact that it was just as different for them to have another kid around as it was for me to be around them. From time to time, we were left on our own, especially when both Gabe and my mother were working the same shift. It was during one of these times that the boys were playing around in a storage closet that they had been told to stay out of. They were fooling around inside the closet with the door closed, and somehow, they managed to kick the sliding door off its tracks. I just happened to be standing outside the closet at that very moment, and as the door flew off, it fell straight down and caught me in the face. The spring-loaded metal pin that was recessed in the top of the closet door caught me just below my right eye, cutting deeply into my face. Once again, I found myself in a situation where I was injured, and there was no one to take care of me. I had no one to take me to the hospital for stitches. When my mother and Gabe arrived home later that evening, the boys didn't even get into any trouble for what had happened. In spite of the injury to my face, I was told that it would heal, and I was never taken to the hospital for stitches. While it has taken many years, the physical scar on my face has diminished, as have the emotional scars caused by a mother who did not care.

As Gabe continued to sexually abuse me, I became more and more terrified of being left at home with him. Inwardly, I knew that what he was doing was wrong, and when my fear of him became greater than my fear of my mother, I finally decided to tell her what was going on. One night when she came home from work, I was able to get her aside and tell her everything that had been going on. She listened to what I had to say, but she made it quite clear that she didn't believe me; she was in complete denial, believing that Gabe wasn't capable of doing something like that to me. Later that night, when all of us kids were in bed, she confronted Gabe, who obviously denied everything and made me out to be a little liar and a troublemaker. My mother's response to his denial was to come upstairs to my room, where she dragged me out of bed and slapped me around while telling me that the situation was entirely my fault. Things between my mother and Gabe were never quite the same after that incident, and it wasn't long after that they went their separate ways. From what I have been able to find out, the parting of the ways was instigated by Gabe. He justified his actions by saying that I was nothing but trouble and that it would just be a matter of time before I made some more irrational claims of abuse.

My mother now decided that it was in her best interest to return to Toronto, so we did just that, renting a small basement apartment just off the Danforth. For the longest time, my mother blamed me for breaking up her relationship with Gabe, and at every opportunity, she would remind me that it was my fault. I was told time and time again that I alone was the sole cause of her unhappiness and that I alone was responsible for the fact that she was once again on her own. In spite of her complaining, it wasn't long before my mother was back in the saddle again, and there followed what seemed to be an endless string of male friends.

4

Why Am I Here?

I spent the next few months living under a cloud of guilt and shame while frequently being reminded by my mother that I was the sole cause of all of her problems. She was like a broken record. She just kept on and on and on about me being the cause of her breakup with Gabe. With no end in sight to her whining and complaining, I made the conscious decision to try and redeem myself. In spite of being innocent of any wrongdoing, I made it my job to take advantage of every opportunity I could to do things for her. I figured that by doing things for her. I would earn some favor and maybe even receive some positive recognition for my efforts.

One afternoon I arrived home from school to find a package of pork chops sitting out on the kitchen counter. My plan was coming together, and as I stood there in the kitchen, I saw it unfolding before my eyes. I was going to take a shot and take advantage of the situation that had been presented to me by preparing them for my mother. Since I had often watched her prepare pork chops, I felt very confident that I knew exactly what to do and how to do it. So, I began to cook them exactly how I remembered her doing it and began by placing the pork chops in a frying pan with the stove element set on simmer. I slowly browned them on both sides, after which I added a small amount of water to the pan. I remember feeling really good about how well everything was going, not realizing just how quickly my plan was about to fall apart. I made one fatal mistake. Instead of leaving the pork chops simmering, I turned the element off. Believing that I had done everything correctly, that I had done everything exactly the same way my mother did it, I sat down in front of the TV, waiting for her to come home.

I remember being quite excited at the prospect of her arrival, and I didn't have to wait too long until I heard the door open. At last, she was home, but surprise, surprise, she was not alone. She had company with her, having brought home the new man in her life with the intention of cooking dinner for him, hence the reason the pork chops were out on the counter. When she saw that I had attempted to cook the pork chops and that my efforts had been unsuccessful, she was absolutely furious with me for ruining her dinner plans. As only my mother could, she destroyed me with every word that came out of her mouth; she told me that I was useless, hopeless, pathetic, stupid, etc. It seemed as if the list was endless. As for me, not only was I very upset at the fact that once again I had failed her, I was extremely embarrassed that she had berated me in such a manner in front of her new boyfriend.

My mother had befriended one of her co-workers and, in conversation with her, had shared with her that she would really like to quit drinking. It turned out that her co-worker was a former alcoholic who had gone through the Twelve Step Program with Alcoholics Anonymous. After exchanging their life experiences, my mother was invited to accompany her co-worker to her weekly A.A. meeting. It was quite a surprise to me when my mother became a regular attendee at the weekly meetings; at long last, she now had the support of others to help her quit drinking. I recall one very special evening when she took me along with her to an A.A. meeting. During the meeting, I was left to play quietly in a back room where, using a pencil and paper, I made a tracing of my hand and cut it out using a pair of scissors. I then wrote a different comment on each finger of the hand. On the first finger, I wrote, "To my mommy who doesn't drink." On the second finger, I wrote, "To the mom I love." On the third finger, I wrote, "Sober at last." On the fourth finger, I wrote, "I love you, Mom." On the fifth and last, I wrote, "Finally free." Without understanding the significance of what I had written after the meeting that night, I gave the cut-out hand to my mother. It was one of the few things that I ever gave her that she considered valuable enough to keep. She actually kept it for over twenty-five years. Now that the drinking had stopped, I had great expectations of my mother; I actually believed that this was a life-changing experience for her and that it would cause her to begin to treat me differently. You cannot imagine how disappointed I felt when I came to the realization that very little had changed. For my mother, it was business as usual as she still continued to leave me home alone. The need she once had to go out and drink had been replaced by her need to have a man in her life.

Some months earlier, when we had first moved to Toronto, my mother had applied for subsidized housing and had her name placed on the waiting list at Ontario Housing. I'm not sure whether it was shock or relief that was all over her face when she received a call to inform her that an apartment had become available in the Lawrence Avenue area. She went and checked out the apartment and decided to take it, so once again, we moved, and once again, I had to change schools. Because of all the upset in our lives, the moves in London, then from London to Toronto, and now from the Danforth up to Lawrence Avenue, my grade four results were far from stellar. After moving into the apartment on Lawrence Avenue, my mother registered me in the local school where the principal, after reviewing my report card, would only allow me to start grade five on probation. Whether I was allowed to stay in grade five or not would depend on my ability to handle the work. I was so fortunate to be blessed with a great teacher who took me under his wing, and he helped me through a very difficult transition. Being allowed to start grade five opened up a number of new opportunities for me, one of which was track and field. I discovered very quickly that I was well suited to a number of different events, and, over the school year, I participated in a number of track meets where I won several ribbons and medals. In spite of my success in track and field, there was no recognition of my efforts or my accomplishments by my mother. As for her, she had found a job working at St. Michaels Detoxification Centre, which was way downtown from where we lived. It required her to take a long bus ride to and from work, and this, combined with the different shifts she had to work, did little to improve her temperament. She was angry and miserable all the time, angry and miserable with everyone and everything, and it was absolutely impossible to please her. She continued to run me down at every opportunity. It didn't matter what I did, it was never good enough. For example, if I didn't clean my bedroom up to her expectations, she would tell me that I was a pig and no one would ever want me as a wife. On every occasion that I ever had trouble with something at school, she would be sure to tell me that I was stupid and would never get anywhere in life. It got to the point that I came to believe that she hated me. She obviously didn't love me; you don't treat someone you love the way she treated me.

It wasn't long before the Christmas season was with us again, and I had been saving every nickel I could to buy my mother a very special gift. I had my eye on a chip and dip bowl that I had seen in one of the local stores and was so happy that I had been able to save up enough money to buy it for her. One day, a couple of weeks before Christmas, I rushed straight home after school so that I could do my shopping. I made my way to the store where I purchased the chip and dip bowl for my mother, managing to get it home before she arrived home from work. I wrapped up her gift in the nice Christmas paper that I had bought, and I placed it under our Christmas tree. I was so happy that I had been able to buy my mother something special, and I desperately hoped that it would please her. I hoped that it would not only make her happy but that it would maybe even change her attitude toward me. One night, a few days before Christmas, my mother arrived home from work in a lousy mood. When she would get this way, she would prowl around the apartment, looking for any small detail that did not meet with her approval. On this particular evening, she decided to focus on the condition of my bedroom, which I was expected to clean up every day after coming home from school. When she had completed her inspection, she flew into a furious rage, obviously not very satisfied with my efforts. She came storming out of my room and headed straight for the Christmas tree, and picked up the present I had bought for her.

While holding my Christmas gift to her in her hands, she told me that she didn't want anything from a kid like me, after which she threw it on the floor, where it was smashed into pieces. I really can't put into words the hurt that I felt at that time. Once again, my heart was broken, once again, I was left wondering why my mother hated me so much. I just couldn't understand why she was so mean to me; I didn't understand why she didn't love me. After all, what had I ever done to her but love her? In spite of how she treated me, I loved my mother with unconditional love. I remember often thinking to myself that I didn't ask to be born, especially when the person that gave birth to me absolutely hated and despised me. Time and time again, my mother would leave me wounded, shattered, and broken, leaving me asking myself, "Why am I here?"

With Christmas and New Year out of the way, it seemed like the next few months just flew by, and before I knew it, it was April already. Once again, my mother made the announcement that we were on the move, this time to a bigger apartment unit located at Teesdale in Scarborough. Although my situation at home really hadn't changed a whole lot, with the better weather and longer days, I actually felt that things were improving. I had successfully completed grade five at school, and after having a great summer break which passed too quickly, I found myself facing a brand-new school year. I had worked very hard and had managed to get a passing mark that enabled me to enter grade six. With this success behind me, I began my new school year with an abundance of optimism and great expectations.

It wasn't long before my world was shaken to the core once again when I experienced a situation where my optimism and expectations were severely challenged. Early in the new school year, I had the opportunity to go on a school camping trip, an experience that just reinforced what I already knew, that I was in serious lack. When I was changing my clothes at the camp, the other kids saw the condition of my one and only bra, which was stretched and torn. They saw the holes in my socks, and they saw the pulls and tugs in my red polyester pants. I couldn't help but hear them whispering and talking about the condition of my clothes, and I became very self-conscious and extremely embarrassed about my appearance. Although my mother always seemed to have enough money to dress very well, she continued to dress me in secondhand rags, which she picked up from the used clothing store or from Goodwill.

The month of October finally came around, and now that I had turned eleven years of age, it was like someone had flicked a switch, causing things to change in my body. It just seemed to happen overnight. My body shape changed, and my chest began to develop quickly. So quickly, in fact, that in a very short time, my mother realized that my chest was bigger than hers, a fact that seemed to get her very upset. While she continued to buy herself new clothing to add to her wardrobe, I continued to wear whatever she picked up for me from Goodwill or the used clothing store. It was the butterfly and moth analogy. My mother needed to dress well to attract the men, and since I had no value in her eyes, it didn't matter how I looked. As my body developed, I only became more self-conscious of my appearance and more embarrassed about my lack of decent clothing. After the camp experience, things just seemed to go downhill for me when I had a bad accident in the kitchen. In my eagerness to help my mother and make a good impression on her, I knocked a pot of boiling potatoes off the stove. The result was that I badly burned my right leg, and, in spite of my leg being bandaged for six weeks, my mother still expected me to do all the housework.

A few weeks after my birthday, I was at home alone with Bill, the new man in my mother's life. Strangely enough, my mother seemed to think that it was okay for her to leave me home alone with all these men that she would bring home. It happened on a Saturday afternoon when my mother was at work; Bill looked at me and made a comment to me about the condition of the clothes that I was wearing. He said, "You and I need to go on a shopping spree." So, at his direction, we got ready and headed over to the mall. After window shopping and checking out a few stores, Bill finally made his choice and bought me a gorgeous pink jean pantsuit that cost $50 and looked absolutely great on me. I was so naive at the time that I believed that Bill was just taking pity on me, having no idea that Bill had other plans, no idea of the true motive behind his buying me the jean pantsuit. On the way home from the mall, we stopped at the local grocery store to pick up a few things that we needed for dinner that night. On our arrival back at the apartment, before I began to put away the groceries, I once again thanked Bill very much for buying me the pantsuit. As I was putting some items away in the fridge, Bill came up behind me, wrapped his arms around me, and grabbed my breasts. I mustered all of my strength and managed to push myself away from him, thinking that having done this, he would stop, but he just kept coming after me. To avoid him, I moved into the living room, but he just followed me and grabbed me again, and this time he tried to kiss me. But I was ready for him and managed to push him back, pushing him so hard that he fell over the rocking chair. At this, Bill got the message and finally stopped his advances and left me alone. Based on Bill's actions, I put two and two together and came up with the conclusion that Bill and my mother must be having difficulties in their relationship. Why else would Bill be pursuing me? Thankfully, a short time after this incident, my mother and Bill stopped seeing each other and went their separate ways. I never did tell her about Bill's advances or about what happened that Saturday; I guess I was just afraid of once again being blamed for her losing her man.

About a month or so after Bill had left the scene, my mother informed me that she had been to see a plastic surgeon and that she was going to have some work done. Based on the fact that she had too many wrinkles on her face that were making her look old, she had made the decision to have a facelift. This would be the first of three facelifts she would have in her lifetime, and since she didn't want anyone to know about her surgery, she had scheduled her vacation to coincide with her surgical procedure. On the day of the surgery, I accompanied her to the clinic, where I sat waiting for hours until the procedure was complete and she was out of recovery. When the nurse helped her from the recovery area back into the waiting room, I was shocked at her appearance as they had her head wrapped up like a mummy. The nurse called a cab for us, and I got my mother home and tucked her into her bed to begin the recovery process. Although I was only eleven years of age, I spent the next three weeks taking care of her every need, washing the caked blood out of her hair, changing her dressings, making her meals, and so on. I became her personal attendant, her orderly, and her slave, jumping to attention in response to her every command. Through this constant need for my assistance, the message that I received was that it was all about her and nothing about me. It's no wonder that I often asked myself, "Why am I here?"

5

Boarding House Blues

With my mother, all healed up and back in the dating game, Christmas and New Year over with, the balance of my time in grade six was quite uneventful and passed very quickly. Before I knew it, summer break had come and gone, and I now found myself entering grade seven at Samuel Hearn Jr. High. A week or so after the beginning of the school year, I met my first love, a young man by the name of George. George lived on the tenth floor of the same apartment building that my mother and I lived in, and we first met when I babysat for his sister. Even though he was much older than I, he was sixteen, and I was only twelve. We had an instant connection when we met. George basically gave me everything that I didn't get at home; he gave me his time, his attention, his respect, his love and compassion, and so much more.

As a child of neglect, I was totally open to what he gave me because what he gave me was everything that I yearned for and longed to receive from my mother. Although George gave me what I was looking for, he also exposed me to other things that would cause me some issues down the road. It was George who got me started on cigarettes, and when one thing led to another, he was the one that introduced me to sex. Based on my experience at this time in my life, I truly had a distorted view of what love was. I continued to have problems at school because of my outward appearance, and I was never accepted or well-liked because of it. Very little had changed at home, where I continued to feel totally unloved, where I felt that I was more of an inconvenience to my mother than a blessing to her. I just wanted to be loved. George showed me that he loved me and that he cared for me, so I gave him my all. While George and I were spending all our time together, my mother had been spending all her time with her new boyfriend, a man called Buzz.

The first time I met Buzz was when he arrived home with her early one morning. It was about 2:00 am, and they had been out at a dance. Buzz was very open and very friendly toward me, and he didn't talk down to me or make me feel like I was just a kid. We often talked when he would come over for a coffee with my mother, and I actually looked forward to seeing him. Buzz and my mother went out together for about nine months, and even after they decided to go their separate ways, they still remained friends. From time to time, Buzz would just drop in out of the blue to have a coffee and share some conversation with us. Even though I was still in a relationship with George, Buzz started to visit me frequently in the evenings when my mother was at work. It wasn't long before he became my best friend, and we became quite close, so close in fact, that he taught me how to French kiss at the young age of thirteen.

Once again, my mother had the urge to move, a move that was no doubt motivated by her lengthy travel time to and from work. This time we moved from Teesdale to Broadview & Gerrard, moving from the north end of the city to the downtown area, a move that would give my mother easier access to the subway line. It was shortly after we moved downtown that I found out I was pregnant by George, and, needing someone to confide in, I shared my situation with Buzz. Being absolutely terrified of what my mother might do to me when she found out, I asked Buzz if he would tell my mother for me. Buzz agreed to do just that and was very sympathetic to my condition, telling me not to be scared and that everything would be okay. After pouring my heart out to him and telling him that I was pregnant, Buzz then said that he would like to make love to me, quite the request considering I was thirteen years old and he was forty-six. Since I viewed Buzz as my friend and confidant, since I didn't want to let him down, and since I believed that I owed him so much for helping me, I said, "Yes." Afterwards, I asked Buzz why he had wanted to sleep with me. His answer to me was, "I only loved you. Besides, I couldn't do any more damage." At that time, I truly thought that it was okay because he was my friend, and I trusted him, truly believing that he cared for me and that he loved me. In later years, these very words that were spoken to me by Buzz would come back to haunt me.

In time I would come to see how he had preyed on me by using this situation to take advantage of me and using me for his own gratification. However, at that time, Buzz did remain true to his word, and the following night, he did take my mother out for dinner and told her I was pregnant. I don't know exactly what Buzz said to her, but when my mother arrived home that night, she was very calm and quiet, saying only that it was okay and that she would take care of it. The next day my mother took me to see our doctor, who determined that I was about twelve weeks pregnant. After my mother asked the doctor to make arrangements for me to have a therapeutic abortion at the Toronto General Hospital, we went home. Fortunately, Buzz was there the next day to drive me to and from the hospital, although he did get quite angry when I wouldn't hold his hand. As for my mother, once again, she was absent from the situation, but then she was never ever there for me when I needed her.

We had only been living at Broadview and Gerrard for about six months when once more, my mother made the announcement that we were on the move again. We were always moving, so much so that I honestly felt like a gipsy, never having a chance to put down any roots at all. Apparently, during the time that my mother had been working at St. Michael's Detoxification Centre, she had become aware that there was an acute shortage of living accommodations for alcoholics and drug addicts. My mother decided that she was going to help meet the need; she was going to set up a boarding house that would cater primarily to alcoholics and drug addicts. My mother had gone out and found a large old house located on Queen Street in Toronto, one that was suitable for conversion into a boarding house. After making the purchase and completing some minor renovations, she was open for business, and in a matter of two to three days, she had all the rooms rented out. During the time we lived on Queen Street, my relationship with my mother showed absolutely no sign of improvement. While I continued to live in the hope that she might pay some attention to me, it never happened. It was almost as if she was unable to acknowledge that I even existed. In a last-ditch effort to get some response from my mother, I started to do the craziest things. On one occasion, I deliberately broke my arm by smashing it on an iron railing. You cannot imagine my disappointment when my plan didn't work when the only attention I got was her getting angrier at me by the minute. She was absolutely furious with me because I had a broken arm, and she told me how inconvenient it was going to be for her as it would prevent me from doing all of the housework and cooking the meals for the boarders.

The boarding house soon became a page out of hell for me as I was not only left to cook all the meals for the ten men who lived there, but I also had to do all their laundry as well. Before my mother would go to work each morning, she would only leave out so much food for me to cook, after which she would put a lock on the fridge and on the freezer. The amount of food that she left out never seemed to be enough, and, more often than not, I would go hungry because after serving the boarders, there would be nothing left for me to eat. In later years, I have come to recognize that this was not entirely my mother's doing. Because I truly believed I was worthless and because I felt I was of no value to anyone, I, therefore, subconsciously believed that I didn't deserve to eat. Even though these men were alcoholics and drug addicts, they were men who went out to work every day, so I saw them as having value. Because of my distorted viewpoint, I made sure that they had a good serving of food, even if it was at my expense. All I seemed to do was clean, cook, do laundry, go hungry and fight off the advances of a bunch of alcoholics and drug addicts. This was certainly not the best environment for a thirteen-year-old girl to grow up in, particularly when there was absolutely no support from her one and only parent.

With my busy schedule of school, homework, housework, cooking and laundry, time passed very quickly that year. Before I knew it, summer was over, and I was making the big move into high school. It was during my first semester in high school when it happened. I was hurrying from one class to another when I tripped and fell down, knocking out both my front teeth in the process. When my mother arrived home from work that night, she took one look at the condition of my teeth, shook her head, and walked away. She did take the time later in the evening to tell me that she didn't have the money to get them fixed, and I would have to live with it. You cannot imagine how I felt when later that week, she took me shopping with her to buy herself a new dress. My mother needed a new dress to wear for a party she was going to, and when she found the one she was looking for, it cost her $400, leaving me again feeling totally alienated. After telling me that she didn't have the money to fix my teeth, she had to take me along to see her spending $400 on a new dress. It seemed that my life was just a continuous series of circumstances, events, and situations that provided my mother with every opportunity to show me that I was of absolutely no value.

My only source of stability through all this was none other than Buzz, who continued to come over for visits when my mother was not home. We would have a coffee together and sit and talk about life in general, and since I was taking a hair-cutting course at school, I would sometimes cut his hair. October came along again, and I reached yet another new milestone in my life. I turned fourteen, and having another year under my belt, I now considered myself quite grown up. I am not sure how it came about, but I began to develop an acute interest in my father and at every opportunity, I would ask my mother questions about him. I must have driven her crazy with all my questions, so much so that once again, she tracked my father down. I never did find out how she managed to do it, but she did it. She found out that he had moved to Vancouver, British Columbia. I later found out that my father had been living in Vancouver for about four years, having moved there when I was around ten years old. My mother managed to make contact with him and made arrangements for us to go out to Vancouver for a visit so that I would have an opportunity to see him.

The week before I was scheduled to leave on my big trip, Buzz showed up one night and took me out to the mall and bought me a nice new bikini. I thought it was for me to get some sun while in British Columbia, but he obviously had other ideas, as he said that he would like to get some pictures of me wearing it when I got back. Before we left for British Columbia, I was filled with so many expectations of what it would be like to see my father again. I was also terrified of once again being rejected by him, and I can remember being on the plane, reliving in my mind everything that had happened the last time I saw him. By this time, my mother had told me what he had blurted out when I was born, when he had said, "I didn't want a girl". These words hung over me as an executioner's axe does over the condemned, and of course, I couldn't help but wonder if he still didn't want a girl like me. Strangely enough, my mother actually seemed to be looking forward to the visit. It was almost as if she was looking to renew her relationship with my father.

When the plane landed in Vancouver, I was full of mixed emotions. I just wasn't sure how to respond to my father or how he would respond to me. He met us at the airport and, after loading our luggage in his car, he drove us to his apartment, where he left us alone and went back to work. The whole time we were there, he showed very little interest in me and gave me the impression that he didn't really care that I was around at all. My mother's hopes were also dashed since my father was still drinking while she was not, so they really didn't have much in common anymore. To make matters worse, my father had a lady friend whom he had been seeing for about three years, and we were more of an intrusion than anything else. My mother and I were there for the two longest weeks of our lives, and any glimmer of hope that I ever had of being accepted by my father was totally crushed. I can remember sitting in the plane flying home to Ontario, wishing that I was dead because I didn't even have one parent who loved me.

It was such a relief to be back in Ontario where to escape all the hurt and the emotions that I was feeling, I threw myself into my new nursing course that I was taking at school. The curriculum of the course I was taking included some hands-on training in local nursing homes and hospitals. When it was my turn to go out, I was sent to work in a local nursing home, the Rotary Laughlin Centre. I was truly passionate about the work and had a great desire to provide the best care possible for my patients. I saw how many of these elderly people were neglected and ignored by their families and how many of the nursing home staff mistreated them. After all, I could relate to them because they were just like me. The son of one of the residents at home had been watching me do my work and had recognized my commitment to my patients. He liked how I did my job so much that he hired me to work exclusively with his mother, who just happened to be one of the patients I had under my care. I was in seventh heaven when he offered to hire me as a specialized nurse and informed me that he was prepared to pay the staggering amount of $197/week. Even though the position required me to work ten hours per day, seven days a week, to me, this was like winning the lottery. I figured that by taking on this full-time position at the nursing home. It would help me take my mind off all the emotions and hurt that I was dealing with, especially in the situation with my father.

I quickly came to the realization that taking on a full-time job at the nursing home didn't provide me with the relief that I had expected. I continued to have great difficulty dealing with all the emotional baggage that I was carrying, courtesy of my mother and my father. I had thought that by taking on a full-time job, my work at home would at least diminish, but as far as my mother was concerned, it was business as usual. Despite working ten hours a day, seven days a week at the nursing home, my mother still expected me to come home and cook and clean for the boarders. To my mother, I was just someone to use because, in her eyes, she saw me as a non-person. I surely wasn't her daughter because she treated me like I was her personal slave. I had absolutely no relationship with my mother other than to be there to do all the things that she didn't want to do. I was a time bomb waiting to go off. The clock was ticking, and I was fast approaching the place where I wasn't going to take any more.

When that day did arrive, and it did quite suddenly, I came home from work feeling tired, hungry and alone, and I had had enough. I guess the look on my face said it all because one of the boarders, an aboriginal man named Cherokee, noticed that I was quite distressed. He started talking to me about being bored with Toronto, that it was almost time for him to be going back on the road and do some travelling across Canada. Then he really threw me for a loop when, right out of the blue, he suggested that I should join him and that the two of us should just hit the road and get away from it all. At that time, I was very confused and alone, particularly since Buzz had disappeared off the face of the earth, leaving me with absolutely nobody to talk to. I was about as vulnerable as I could get, feeling totally lost and abandoned, so when Cherokee made the invitation, I figured that I had nothing left to lose. So, I left with him, taking only the clothes on my back and the shoes on my feet. I didn't take time to pack any additional clothing or any of my personal possessions. I embarked on what I thought would be a great adventure, one where I would not have any responsibilities and no one to tell me what to do.

It was still winter and very cold when we left Toronto, and as we hitchhiked across Ontario, it certainly wasn't getting any warmer. In my haste to leave Toronto, I had not dressed appropriately for the weather. I wasn't even wearing boots or a winter jacket, and I had no gloves and no scarf. I had never felt cold like that in my life as we hitchhiked slowly across the country, making our way through London, Dryden, Kenora, Winnipeg, Calgary, Medicine Hat and finally ending up in Vancouver. By the time we reached Vancouver, we had been on the road for thirty-eight days, most of which had been miserable, considering that we had spent most of them cold and hungry. It seemed to me that we had barely survived the experience, living primarily on the coffee that we received at the drop-in centres or the hostels where we stayed overnight. What I found most unusual was the fact that while I was on the road, there were times when I missed my mom, particularly when I was cold, hungry, and scared; after all, I was still only fourteen. Now that Cherokee and I had arrived in Vancouver, I felt that I should make a collect call home just to let my mother know where I was. So, I made the call and spoke with my mother, and I was quite shocked and surprised when I thought I detected some concern in her voice. I was even more surprised when she told me that she was worried about me and that she really wanted me to come home as soon as possible. She asked me to pass the phone to Cherokee so that she could speak to him to tell him that she was not angry with him for taking me on the road. When she spoke to Cherokee, she also told him that it was okay for him to come back to Toronto with me.

Now that our road trip was over and we were cleared to return to Toronto, we had to get our hands on some cash. Cherokee, being well qualified in this area, managed to obtain some fake I.D. that he used to get some money from Social Services. Now that we had some cash in hand, we headed to the nearest restaurant, where we enjoyed our first decent meal in days. Having limited funds, Cherokee said to me that going back by rail was probably the least expensive way for us, so we headed down to the train station, where we bought two one-way tickets to Toronto. Shortly before the train departed, I called my mother again to let her know when we would be arriving in Toronto. The trip back to Toronto was quite uneventful and certainly a whole lot warmer than the trip out to Vancouver.

When we finally arrived at Union Station, we were both quite surprised to see my mother waiting there to meet us. What was even more of a surprise was the fact that she was accompanied by Buzz. It was almost surreal when we walked up to my mother and Buzz and said our hellos because everyone was being so nice to each other. When we finally arrived back at the boarding house and were sharing the highlights of our adventure with my mother and Buzz, the door burst open and in flew four police officers. They had appeared out of nowhere and made a beeline for poor Cherokee. They wrestled him to the floor, placed him under arrest and took him away in handcuffs. That was the last time I ever saw him, and it wasn't until much later that I found out that my mother had him charged with abducting a minor and with sexual assault. The reality was that my mother had lied to us both on the phone. She wanted him in jail, and she wanted me back so that I could become her slave again.

I never did find out at what point my mother realized I was missing or what her initial response was to my disappearance. I hadn't left a note to say that I was leaving or to say where I was going; I just walked out the door and disappeared into the night. Strangely enough, I never did ask her. I guess I really didn't want to know. I didn't want to be disappointed again by possibly finding out that I had been gone a week before she had informed the authorities. Now that my big adventure was over, it was back to the boarding house blues for me. It was like I had never left as I went back to the drudgery of all the household duties. Once again, I was left feeling rejected by my mother and feeling very foolish for having believed that she wanted me back because she truly cared about me. It wasn't long after I had returned from Vancouver that John, another one of my mother's boarders, asked me to leave with him. The boarders all saw how my mother treated me, and, seeing that she placed no value on me, you could hardly blame them for thinking that I was fair game.

While I didn't go on the road with John, I did go for a drive with him on a Sunday afternoon, heading up to Peterborough. While we were driving along, John pulled out a bottle of rye whisky from under the front seat and offered me a drink. I declined his offer, explaining to him that I couldn't drink alcohol as it made me sick. Mumbling something under his breath about me not being able to drink, he opened the bottle and took a long drink, the first of many during the next hour and a half that we were on the road. By the time we reached Peterborough, there wasn't much left in the bottle, and John was, to say the least, quite drunk. When we eventually arrived in downtown Peterborough, he had the misfortune to hit seven parked cars while trying to avoid a fountain that had jumped in front of him. When John's car finally came to a stop, even after the multiple impacts of the collisions, he had only banged his head while I had suffered three cracked ribs.

When the local constabulary arrived on the scene, John's story about the fountain didn't hold water, and he was arrested for drunk driving and taken away to jail. Meanwhile, I was escorted home by two police officers, who explained everything that had happened to my mother. She was furious because I had gone for a drive with John to Peterborough. In fact, she was so mad at me that she called in a worker from Toronto Children's Aid. When the worker arrived at the house, she told him that I was an awful child and that I wouldn't do anything she told me to do. She said I was totally out of control, that she could not control me anymore. She then had the worker put me in a group home for a month, thinking that it would teach me a lesson, that it would straighten me out. At no time during this episode did the worker ask me why I was running!

6

Somebody Loves Me

After completing my month in a group home, I returned home where I found that nothing had changed during my absence. Based on my mother's response to my return and how she was treating me, it was obvious that she still viewed me as a person of no value. A few weeks later, when I had almost reached my saturation point again, I took some much-needed time out of the house. I decided to attend a teen dance at the local high school, where I met Dave, who was the young disc jockey for the dance that night. It was obvious that Dave was attracted to me because, during the evening, he spent an awful lot of time speaking with me. During our conversation, I found out that he had just turned eighteen, and he found out that I was just fourteen. Despite the age difference between us, a mere four years, Dave asked me to go out with him. I said yes, and we quickly became an item. After we had been going out together for about three months, Dave told me that he wanted to marry me and took my hand and placed an engagement ring on my finger. I was completely caught off guard and wasn't quite sure what to say or do. After all, I couldn't very well ask my mother for advice because she would have had a fit. I couldn't even ask Buzz, who was really my only true confidant, because he had found himself a new lady friend and apparently, she was keeping him quite busy. So, for the moment, I never said anything to anybody and, going with the flow, I spent the next six months secretly engaged to Dave. It was almost too good to be true, and it lasted until we had an awful fight one night, which resulted in us going our separate ways. Strangely enough, I can't remember what we fought about; all I remember about that evening was that it was almost a relief to be out of that relationship.

After returning from my cross-Canada adventure, I was very fortunate to get my job back at the nursing home. At that time, it was very important to me that I was still able to earn some money while continuing to build up my nursing credits. Yet another birthday had come and gone, and, despite now being fifteen years old and despite what I had experienced in my life up to that moment in time, I was still seeking a measure of acceptance from my mother. My new plan of attack to win my mother over was to spend all my earnings on her. This concept was based on the fact that she always spent all of her money on her personal wants and desires. I reasoned out in my mind that if I were to spend all my money on her, this would enable her to buy even more of the things she wanted and should certainly earn me some favour. With my plan unfolding, I made up a list of all the things that I thought she would want. It was a long list and included items such as a new freezer, a new vacuum cleaner, a new television, new silverware, and all kinds of stuff. The list was endless.

It only took a few weeks for me to come to the realization that my plan was doomed to fail. This understanding was based on the fact that from my very first purchase, I had not received any recognition or one word of thanks from my mother. On the first occasion that I did go out and buy myself a $15 skirt and a $10 shirt, my mother got terribly upset. In fact, she got downright mad and ugly at me, telling me not to waste my money. The message she sent me was quite clear. It was okay for me to spend my money on her, but if I was spending it on myself, it was a waste. It was becoming more and more obvious to me that I was fighting a losing battle, that no matter what I tried to do to win her approval, nothing would ever be good enough. I had now come to see my mother for who she really was, a mean, angry, selfish, miserable person, and I began to hate and despise her and everything she did.

About the same time Dave and I had broken up, Buzz had reappeared out of the woodwork, having also broken up with his lady friend. Now that he was back on the scene, every day at noon, he would drive over to the nursing home, where he would pick me up and take me out for lunch. One day over lunch, he reached forward and took hold of both of my hands, and, with my hands in his, he asked me not to say anything until he was finished. He said, "Sharon, I don't quite understand what I'm feeling, but it started when you went to Vancouver. I would go to bed thinking of you, I would wake up thinking of you, and I just couldn't get you out of my mind. The only conclusion I can come to is that I have fallen in love with you." The first thought that went through my head was that, at long last, somebody loved me, and it wasn't an issue for me that this person who said he loved me was forty-eight years old, thirty-three years my senior. After this declaration of his love for me, Buzz now began to give me $100 bills which he instructed me to hide under my mattress at home for safekeeping. On the nights when my mother was at work, he would come over to the house and pick me up along with one of the bills, which he used to take me to a motel.

While this was going on, my situation at home was going from bad to worse, with my mother becoming more miserable, angrier and meaner by the day. Buzz was also going through some major changes in his life as he had now decided to officially leave his wife of fourteen years, even though he had been playing the field for most of that time. The next milestone on my journey remains so vivid in my mind that it is just as if it happened yesterday. I can remember getting up that morning and, after getting washed and dressed and making my bed, making my way into the kitchen to grab some breakfast. My mother took one look, and scowled, and barked, "Take out the

*#$! Garbage!" This outburst from her was the last straw for me, and, as so eloquently requested by my mother, I did take out the garbage, and I did so without saying a word. Instead of going back into the house, I just kept walking, leaving behind everything I owned. This was the day that I left home for the last time. As I was walking down the street, I slipped my hand into my pocket and found enough loose change to take a bus over to Buzz's apartment. I felt very confident that he would take care of me, especially since he had told me many times that he loved me, plus the fact that he had been sleeping with me for a number of months.

When I finally arrived at his apartment, I told him I wasn't going back home ever again because I was sick and tired of being mistreated by my mother. At that time, it was very easy for me to justify moving in with Buzz as I just wanted to be loved, and my mother evidently wasn't prepared to do that. I wanted, I needed, someone to take care of me, and my mother wasn't prepared to do that either. Yes, there was a considerable age difference between us, but it didn't seem to matter because Buzz said that he loved me and that he would take care of me. I had only been living with Buzz for a few weeks when he told me that he didn't want me to stay on the birth control pill because it was not good for my health. In a cavalier attitude, he told me, "Don't worry, we'll take our chances," and that's exactly what we did. Everything was going along just fine until the day before my sixteenth birthday when I found out that I was pregnant. When Buzz came home for lunch that day, I gave him the news, and surprisingly, he was far from happy. In fact, he was downright angry and upset. This was hardly the response I had expected from him, and I couldn't understand his upset, particularly since it had been his idea for me to go off the pill in the first place.

He was the one who had told me what to do. He was the one who had said that I was not to worry, and I couldn't help wondering what exactly he expected to happen if neither of us was using any type of contraceptive. About three months after I had walked out on my mother and moved in with Buzz, she bumped into him while picking up some paint at the local paint store. In the ensuing conversation, my mother found out that I was living with Buzz, and she made it quite clear to him that she was not very happy about it. Things went from bad to worse when Buzz came right out and told her I was pregnant and that he was the father. Well, my mother was absolutely furious with him, and her first response was to pick up a gallon can of paint and threaten to kill him with it. Now that she knew where I was, now that she knew my condition, my mother performed one final act of malice toward me. She removed me from her medical coverage, which was the only other thing that she could do to hurt me at that particular time.

In the early days of my pregnancy, I suffered constantly from a migraine-type headache which caused me to experience extreme nausea and vomiting. It was an awful experience for me, draining every ounce of strength I had, leaving me feeling terrible and looking very ragged and tired. When I was about three months into my pregnancy, an incident occurred that would haunt me for the next twenty years. It happened early one Sunday morning with Buzz getting out of bed and taking a shower, after which he got dressed up in his new jacket, shirt, and pants. After brushing his hair and splashing on some cologne, he told me that he was going out as he had arranged to take his ex-wife out to breakfast. I was totally flabbergasted by what I was hearing, and I could not understand why he would be leaving me at home while taking his ex-wife out to breakfast, particularly since we didn't have any groceries in the house. What was even more difficult for me to understand was why he had to get all dressed up in his new clothes and smell nice to do it. Considering the fact that Buzz had played the field while he was married, it was very hard for me not to be suspicious and suspect that he had something else in mind.

When Buzz finally left for breakfast, he was running a bit late. He had only been gone about fifteen minutes or so when the phone rang. I got up out of bed to answer the phone and, when I picked up the phone and said hello, the woman at the other end seemed quite surprised to hear a female voice. She was obviously expecting Buzz to answer the phone, and since there was a female voice at the other end of the line, she asked to speak to Buzz. When I informed her that Buzz was not home and that he had gone out for breakfast, she immediately asked me who she was speaking to. I told her that my name was Sharon and that I was Buzz's girlfriend, a statement that brought the conversation to an abrupt end as she immediately hung up the phone. I later found out that it had been Buzz's ex-wife on the phone and that up to this moment in time, she had not been aware that I was even in the picture. When Buzz eventually arrived at her apartment to pick her up, he received a few choice words from her, after which the apartment door was slammed in his face, putting an end to any plans that he had for the day. Buzz caught me by surprise when he returned home early, and when I asked why he was back so soon, he told me everything that had happened. Then he spoke some words that not only broke my heart but haunted me for years to come. As sick and awful as I looked, Buzz then said to me, "You might as well get dressed; I guess I have to take someone out." I was so distressed by these words that I began to wonder why everyone felt that they had the right to mistreat me, use me and abuse me. After all, I hadn't done anything to deserve this kind of treatment.

No matter what happened to me, I was determined not to make the same mistakes I had seen my mother make, even if it killed me. I had become so accustomed to being mistreated that I came to believe this was all I was ever good for, that this was all that I was ever going to have. So, when Buzz began to treat me just as badly as my mother had all of my life, I just accepted it and hid behind my broken heart, hoping things were going to get better or at least not any worse. One night, seven months into my pregnancy, I was sitting on the edge of my bed when Buzz looked over at me strangely and said, "Do something with your hair. You look awful." It was becoming more evident to me that he was completely oblivious to pregnancy and was ignorant of the fact that I could not wash my own hair because every time I bent my head down, it would cause me to throw up. In many respects, Buzz was becoming a lot like my mother. If it wasn't directly about him, if it did not directly affect him, it was of little consequence to him. As my time of delivery drew closer, I told Buzz that we had to start getting some baby things such as a crib, blankets, diapers and so on. On the day that his income tax refund came in the mail, I got so excited thinking about all the things that we could buy for the baby that I took a bus over to where he was working. I arrived at the site and, with great anticipation, passed Buzz his three-hundred-dollar refund cheque, which he promptly stuffed in his pocket. He then reached into his other pocket and pulled out $3, which he handed to me, saying, "Go to the Salvation Army Store and buy some used sleepers."

When he spoke those words, he may as well have stabbed me in the heart. This time he wasn't just hurting me. This time he was hurting my baby, our baby.

Now that I was almost full term in my pregnancy, my mother had taken it upon herself to contact my father in British Columbia just to let him know what was going on. While it made absolutely no sense for her to do this, particularly since we had not had any contact with him for years, she obviously believed that it would cause Buzz and me some problems. She had also given my father our telephone number, and when the telephone rang, and I answered it, I was more than surprised to find my father on the other end of the line. Out of everything that he had to say, all that I can remember of that call was my father saying to me, "I am going to kill him," and, "How is it, Sharon, that you could have done something so stupid?" When I asked my father where he was calling from, he did not reply, leaving me with the belief that he was already in Toronto. I was terrified, and, knowing what my father was capable of doing, I quickly hung up the phone and called Buzz at work and gave him the general content of my father's call. While I packed enough clothes for us to last a week or so, Buzz dropped everything he was doing and rushed straight home, and then we headed out of town. Buzz drove us out to Oshawa, where his mother had a small basement apartment, and that's where we hid out for the next month or so. It was quite uncomfortable for me there as Buzz's mother made it perfectly clear that she did not like me at all. In fact, I felt she hated me.

In retrospect, she probably hated the circumstances that her son had chosen to create, that a man of his years had taken advantage of a child the way he had done. Thankfully, my father never did show up in Toronto since Libby, his new wife, had convinced him that he had no right to get involved as he had been out of my life too long. When Buzz and I finally returned home, I called my mother and spoke with her on the phone to find out what was happening. She told me that she had spoken with my father, who had told her that there was nothing that he could do to change anything and, therefore, there wasn't any point in him coming. If we had not panicked and rushed to Oshawa, if we had only stayed put in Toronto, we would have received the second call that my father made. Apparently, my father had called back to let us know that he was not coming to Toronto, but we weren't home to take his call. We had already gone.

A couple of weeks after returning home from Oshawa, I received a call from my mother to tell me that something had arrived in the mail for me. She then told me that my father had sent me a cheque, but before she would tell me the amount, I would have to agree to give her half the money. Not that I received a lot of mail, but any mail I did receive was always opened by my mother, who felt it was her right. My mother then told me she felt that she was entitled to half of it because she had been the one who always supported me, while my father had never paid her any child support. She finished her negotiations by stating, "If you don't agree to my terms, you won't get any of the money at all." My mother was quite serious when she said this, as she was more than capable of forging my signature and cashing the cheque, and that is exactly what she did. I never did see the cheque my father sent me. As I expected, she forged my name and cashed the cheque, leaving my half for pick-up at the local paint shop where I knew the owner. Even though my mother knew that my father had sent the money for my baby and not for me, once again, her greed came first. Since Buzz wasn't coming through with any money, I really had no choice but to agree to my mother's terms, as the half was better than nothing. As my due date approached, Buzz finally decided to put some effort into finding a used crib, eventually finding one at a garage sale, which he brought home and gave a coat of paint. As for the other items, such as diapers, formula, sleepers etc., I do believe that Buzz thought they were all going to appear out of nowhere because he certainly wasn't out at the store picking them up.

The night my labour began, there was a major storm raging across southern Ontario. When my labour pains were down to less than 5 minutes apart, Buzz finally drove me to the hospital. The windshield wipers on his van were not working, and it was truly a miracle that we made it to the hospital safely, considering that we had to drive through a torrential rainstorm to get there. It wasn't long before I was in difficult labour, and when Buzz saw the pain that I was in, he looked at me and said, "I would never have done this if I had known it was going to be like this." After forty-two hours of labour, our son Chris was born at 10:58 am on 1st July 1980, weighing in at 8 lbs. 2 oz. Unfortunately, Buzz missed out on the arrival of his new son as he had gone home to shower and change. After spending a couple of days in the hospital, I was finally allowed to go home with our baby, so Buzz picked us up at the hospital and dropped us off at the apartment.

On arriving home, I quickly took stock of what I had for the baby and soon realized that I was missing many things. I didn't even have any diapers. Thank God I was breastfeeding, which meant that I didn't have to worry about a baby formula for at least two weeks or until I dried up. When Chris was five weeks old, I had no choice but to go out and find a job in another nursing home in order to bring in some money to buy what he required. For whatever reason, Buzz seemed oblivious to the fact that his son required diapers and formula and was having great difficulty providing the finances to purchase these necessities. As for my mother, she never came to the hospital, she never even called me on the phone, she didn't send a card, she didn't send flowers, and she didn't even send her grandson a small soft toy like a teddy bear. I felt quite foolish for having expected my mother to change now that she had a grandson, especially since all the indicators pointed to her being as good a grandmother as she had been a mother. "Not!"

7

Only Good for Work and Sex

My job search turned out to be very successful, and I was able to find a job in another nursing home. I had only been back to work for about a week when Buzz took it upon himself to set up a meeting between my mother, my nanny and myself. The meeting was scheduled to take place at my mother's house, and I was quite excited about it as it would give them both an opportunity to see Chris, who was now almost six weeks old. While Buzz drove me over to my mother's house for the meeting, he did not come in but waited outside in the van with the engine running, ready to move should I need to make a quick exit. Before I stepped out of the van with Chris, Buzz told me that if I didn't come out of the house in twenty minutes or less, he would come in and get me. To further emphasize how serious he was, he said that, if required, he would drive the van through the front door. Having made an impression on me, I was going to make it out on time as I really didn't want to find out if Buzz meant what he said. While the meeting with my mother and my nanny was cordial, none of the issues that my mother had with me were ever addressed. With nothing changing and everything remaining the same, we just continued back on the same old merry-go-round, going around the mountain one more time.

Thankfully, the nausea and the headaches I had experienced during my pregnancy left immediately after Chris was born. Now that it had been a couple of months since giving birth, I had my figure back, and I was feeling very good about that. Buzz also felt very good about it and, liking what he saw, he suddenly became very interested and very fussy about how I dressed for him. Short skirts, tight T-shirts and high heels became the order of the day. At the weekends, Buzz would get me to dress up, and then we would go for a walk down Yonge Street, or perhaps I should say he had me strut down Yonge Street. It was during one of these walks with Buzz that a man who was sitting on a bench shouted over at me, "Hey Baby, I'll give you fifty bucks." Even though we continued walking, I waited for Buzz to respond to the man's remark, or should I say proposition, but he just ignored him and said nothing. Since Buzz wasn't going to protect what was left of my honour, I came to my own defence and told the man exactly what he could do with himself. This incident made me realize that Buzz took me out walking because it made him look good. As we walked down the street, other men would look and see this forty-nine-year-old man with a sixteen-year-old girl dressed like a hooker. Buzz was parading his trophy in front of all the other men, and he was enjoying every minute of their envy and their speculation about what he was doing to me.

To save some money, Buzz and I had moved out of his hi-rise apartment into a less expensive duplex apartment, where we rented both the main floor and the basement level. We quickly found out why the rent was so low. It was because the basement flooded every time it rained, and, on top of that, the whole building was infested with mice. Every time we used our shower, which was located in the basement, we could hear the mice running across the roof of the shower; they were everywhere you looked. Concerned about the health issues and how they might affect our son, we went out to the store and bought three dozen mousetraps, and, in one evening, we caught and disposed of eighteen mice. It didn't seem to matter how many mice we caught and killed. They just kept coming. They were breeding faster than we were killing them. Due to our financial situation at that time, we were unable to move anywhere else, so we had no choice but to tough it out for a while. Our son, Chris, was now thirteen months old, and he had become a very busy little boy, constantly getting into places he wasn't supposed to be. During one of his adventures, he ran into the kitchen, grabbed the cord of the kettle, and pulled it off of the counter, spilling the scalding hot water all over his leg. I immediately swooped him up and ran cold water over his leg, and then after wrapping it in a wet towel, I rushed him to the hospital. I spent the next two weeks with Chris at the hospital. Buzz was noticeably absent, and I honestly have no recollection of him coming to visit his son while he was there. I do know that the day Chris was released from the hospital, Buzz wouldn't take the time to come and pick us up, and I had to call my nanny to take us home.

I now began to find myself being left home alone with my son every night while Buzz would go out to his A.A. meetings. At least that's where he said he was going. All I seemed to be good for was performing household duties and, of course, sex, which he always wanted when he got home from his meetings. On the occasions when I was privileged enough to be in his company, he would always flirt with other women. He frequently talked about his previous girlfriends and what he had done with them, knowing good and well that it would either upset me or make me jealous. As time went on, Buzz shared all of his exploits with me, and it was during this expose' of his life that I found out that he had been married twice before, not once as I had previously been led to believe. After telling me how his drinking had destroyed his first marriage, he then shared with me the story of how he had left his first wife and family. Showing absolutely no remorse whatsoever, he told me that he had left home one day to get a loaf of bread and never returned, abandoning his wife and three children, all of whom were under the age of five. Then he also told me that he had another child with a woman he had been with while living in New Brunswick and that they, too, had been left behind. I couldn't help but think that Chris and I might be next!

While I was struggling to deal with all of the garbage that was going on at home, my work situation was also causing me undue stress. I had recently changed jobs, moving to a new nursing home where I felt I would have a greater opportunity for advancement. It didn't take long for me to become aware of the fact that many of the patients were being physically and mentally abused by some of the staff. I got so upset at what I saw happening and, having no control over it and no means of proving to the authorities what I saw happening. I just quit my job. In many respects, I was living what I saw these patients going through day after day, and for me to see someone else going through it was just too much for me to handle. As strange as it may seem, my mother's attitude towards me changed considerably during the first two years of Chris' life, and our relationship improved. While she was visiting us one day, she told us that she was having great difficulty paying her mortgage and was considering finding herself an apartment. Since she didn't want to lose her house, she had a couple of options, one of which was to rent out the house and the other she wanted to run by us. Knowing the condition of the duplex we were living in, she proposed to us that we move into her home and pay the mortgage in lieu of rent. It seemed like a great idea at the time because it was beneficial for all of us. We were desperate to get out of the duplex, and she didn't want to lose the equity in her house. We accepted her offer and immediately called and made a complaint to the Board of Health. This resulted in the duplex being condemned due to it being found unfit for human habitation. Before moving into my mother's house, Buzz had specifically asked her to guarantee that we would be able to stay in it for at least a couple of years, and the answer he received was, "Yes."

About a month after we moved into my mother's house, Buzz received a phone call from his son, who was now living in Edmonton. He was calling to let him know that he was getting married and that he would like him to come to the wedding. Despite having abandoned his wife and family years before and having had no contact with them till now, Buzz actually accepted the invitation and began to make plans for his trip out west. Since family reunions seemed to be in the air, and with Buzz now going to Edmonton for the week, it seemed to me that I might as well go to Vancouver and try and patch things up with my father. So, I plucked up enough courage to call my father and ask him if he would like to meet his grandson. No one was more surprised than I at his response when, without any hesitation, he said, "Yes." So we could travel and return from Toronto airport together, Buzz and I scheduled our flights for the same days and our departure and arrival times as close together as possible. Everything was going according to plan until somewhere between home and the airport parking lot, I lost my purse, which contained all $200 of my travelling money, as well as all my I.D.

Buzz was far from sympathetic to what had happened, and he my circumstances, considering it to be very little short of stupid. So, when he left on his flight to Edmonton, he left with all his money, and when I left on my flight to Vancouver, I left with nothing. The fact that I was going to meet my father was stressful enough for me, but to arrive penniless was downright embarrassing, and I couldn't help but wonder what my father and his wife, Libby, would think. They both met me at the airport, and their response to our arrival was overwhelming, beyond my wildest dreams. They welcomed us with open arms and were both very excited and thrilled to meet little Chris, behaving the way that doting grandparents do. I saw a side of my father that I had never seen before. When we finally arrived at my father's apartment, I walked through the door into a room that was full of red roses, all for me. I was totally overwhelmed by their warm welcome. When my suitcase appeared on the carousel at the airport in Vancouver, it burst open and looked as if it had been kicked all the way to Vancouver. My father had taken one look at it and said it was questionable that it would make the trip back to Toronto. The next day he took me to a luggage store where he bought me a very expensive new suitcase. We left the luggage store and headed to a children's store, where he bought little Chris a potty chair as I had begun to potty train him shortly before making the trip out west. My father and Libby treated both Chris and me like gold, and it was hard to imagine that he had once hurt me so badly. It was also hard to imagine that months previously, he had threatened to kill Buzz. We had a great visit with my father and Libby, but, like all great visits, it came to an end too soon, and before I knew it, it was time to return to Toronto.

Having arrived back in Toronto after spending a very busy week out west, Buzz and I were both looking for some peace and quiet as we needed a vacation from our vacation. Our peace and quiet was short-lived when we received a phone call from my mother, calling to let us know that she had decided to sell her house, even though she had promised us that we had at least two years before she would do so. Once again, my mother had broken her word. Once again, she was running true to form by doing what suited her, doing what she considered to be in her best interest. She had used us to save her bacon when she could not meet her mortgage payment, and, now that she had her affordable apartment, she was kicking us out. I was absolutely devastated and furious with myself for having trusted my mother. I should have known better. I should have realized that she was doing nothing more than using us to meet her own selfish needs. She had seen the conditions we were living in, knew that we wanted to move, and then played us like an old banjo. At no time did she ever show any regret or remorse for her actions, no concern for her grandson or us.

While waiting for her house to sell, I started bugging Buzz again about letting me work with him in his painting business. Right off the bat, Buzz wasn't too keen on the idea, and he told me that he didn't think any of his customers would look favourably on a woman working in the painting field. Buzz finally agreed to take me on as an apprentice, once again putting me in a position where I had to prove myself, and it wasn't long before his customers spent more time dealing with me than with him. When Buzz finally acknowledged that I was more than capable of doing the work, he made a gesture that only he could by buying me a 2½" sash tool and a 3" Hamilton paintbrush for my eighteenth birthday. When most people receive a birthday gift from a loved one, they usually receive something of a personal nature. Buzz just equipped me for the work because that's where his heart was. It didn't take very long for my mother's house to sell, and before we knew it, we only had a month to find a place to live. As usual, Buzz took the relaxed approach to pack up for the move and finding us a place to live, which meant that he left it all to me. Now that we were on a deadline, I contacted a real estate agent who was able to find me a small bungalow in West Hill, one that we could rent with the option to buy.

The move from my mother's house to the bungalow went well, and although the first year was financially quite difficult, my desire to purchase never waned. It would take a couple of years for us to generate the deposit required and, to get our credit rating cleaned up before we would be able to purchase the bungalow. We eventually purchased the bungalow for ninety-six thousand dollars, which at that time was a huge sum of money. The painting business was booming, and Buzz and I were working day and night on both private and contract jobs, and at times we were hard-pressed to keep up with the workload. We were extremely fortunate to be on contract with a large company, one that was responsible for the painting and decorating of all the Simpson's department stores in the Toronto area. One morning, in the middle of winter, we arrived home after working twenty-two hours straight, having painted the ceiling on one floor of one of the department stores. Being exhausted, we both literally stumbled in through the front door and into bed. We hadn't been there more than twenty minutes when the doorbell rang. I got out of bed, threw on my robe and made my way to the front door to see who was there. When I opened the door, I came face to face with a serviceman from Consumers Gas, who politely informed me that he was there to shut off our gas supply due to non-payment of our account.

Once again, we fell victim to Buzz's lackadaisical attitude toward billing for work done and collection of money owed, which now left us in the position of having no heat in the middle of winter. After showing the Consumers Gas serviceman where the gas shut-off was located, I asked him to please shut the door behind him on his way out and then left him to do what he had to do. I made my way back to the bedroom and sat down on the edge of the bed, not quite sure what to do next. When Buzz asked me who was at the door, I told him what had happened and that we now had no heat as our gas had been shut off. Buzz's only response was, "Oh, Honey, I'm really not interested in having sex right now." He never took the issue of the gas being shut off seriously. He brought it back to his priority. He brought it back to sex! After sleeping for a few hours, Buzz got out of bed and left to pick up a cheque for a portion of the money that was owed to us, enabling us to get the gas turned back on.

Having gone through this very difficult situation, there was certainly a greater focus on billing for work done and following up on the payments. This resulted in the finances coming in more regularly, which allowed us to get caught up on all our outstanding bills, even to the point of us being in the position of having some free cash. With some of our freed-up cash in hand, I took it upon myself to go out and buy Buzz a Commodore 64, as he had been hinting to me for some time that he would like to have a computer so that he could learn to do some programming. The level of work continued for us, and for the next five months, if Buzz wasn't painting, he was on his computer. As soon as he arrived home from work, he would head straight for his computer and remain there, only leaving it to go to the washroom, to eat or to go to bed. Chris and I were totally abandoned. It was as if we didn't exist, and while poor little Chris got no attention at all, the only attention I ever got was when he came to bed looking for sex. Having no understanding of why Buzz would do this to us, I became so stressed out about what was happening that I became anorexic, with my body weight dropping to 118 lbs. and my waist shrinking to 21 inches. As my physical condition worsened, so did my mental state, and I found myself rocking myself back and forth on the couch while he was busy playing on his computer. Buzz was so engrossed with his new toy that he never did notice that I was physically sick and that my mental condition was on a downward spiral or that my self-esteem had hit rock bottom to the point that despair had flooded in.

After living this way for almost five months and spending all of those weeks being ignored, I was now totally convinced that he viewed me as only good for work and sex. What was I to do? Then something changed with Buzz that only reinforced what I now believed when, right out of the blue, he began to bring me home sexy outfits to wear to bed. It now appeared that Buzz needed a little something extra to get himself turned on, and it didn't stop there. Next came his need to take nude photographs of me, photographs that he would keep in his wallet so that he could look at them when the urge arose. I now felt totally degraded, and, having finally reached the point where I wasn't prepared to take it anymore, I decided to tell Buzz that we were finished. So, one day when we were on our way home from work, I broke down and told him I was leaving. Buzz finally got the wake-up call that he never expected, the one that he never thought I would be able to deliver.

When we arrived home, he waited until I had settled down a bit before he asked me why I wanted to leave. This was not the question to ask me at that time, as it only enraged me more. Due to the fact, he was totally oblivious to what was going on around him, he had to ask me such a dumb question. I didn't want to hurt Buzz. I just wanted to kill him. But instead of killing him, I resorted to throwing a cup of coffee at him. The cup, filled with coffee, bounced off the wall and smashed to smithereens, spilling coffee all over his precious computer. This caused a huge argument, and, in a rage, I smashed my hand numerous times on the coffee table, crushing the ring on my finger in the process. Once again, the hurt and the pain I felt on the inside just overwhelmed me, driving me to the point that it felt like a raging inferno. It wouldn't go away, and I just wanted to die. Fortunately for me, a family friend was at home that evening, and he was able to cut the ring off my finger using a pair of pliers and a file.

After this big blow-up, everything seemed to settle down back into the same old rut, and life became bearable for me, far from normal, just bearable. Business continued to be good, and, for the next eighteen months, Buzz and I continued to work on contracts, still painting the huge Simpson's store in downtown Toronto. As time passed, the scope of my involvement in the company expanded to the point where I assumed total responsibility for running our large crew of painters. Since we were required to work seven days a week to maintain the schedule set by the store, the juggling of the crew and the allocating of work was extensive. Over and above this, I was also ordering the paint and supplies, and, when required, I met with the contractor and the Simpson's representative. Because I had taken on such a heavy workload, Buzz adopted the relaxed approach, and since I was basically doing everything, it wasn't long before I became quite exhausted. I remember quite well the day I told Buzz that I was going three ends against the middle and that I couldn't keep up the pace for much longer. I reminded him of all that I was doing, managing the business, cutting the lawn, doing housework, doing the laundry, being a mom, and so much more. Buzz's reply to me was, "Take a day off and do the housework." My response was to hire a housekeeper while I continued to work.

At long last, there had been a shift in my way of thinking and for the first time in my life, I was now stepping out and taking some control over what was happening in my own life. Having proven my ability to manage the business, my self-esteem was elevated to a new level, and my self-confidence greatly increased. One of the first major decisions I made on my own was to go out and buy my first new car, a Mazda 323, and she was a beauty. Feeling a little guilty for having a new car when Buzz didn't, so he wouldn't feel slighted, I bought him a Mazda B2000 pickup truck.

The original driving force behind my becoming a painter was to make money but now that I was very successful in the field, I realized it wasn't really what I wanted to do. I wanted to get out of painting together so I could go back to my first love and pursue a nursing career. When I finally approached Buzz to talk to him about going back to school and finishing my nursing degree, he immediately said that we couldn't afford to have him out of work for two years. In addition to becoming dependent on my income, Buzz had now begun to recognize my value as a painter and as manager of the company. Under my management, the company was growing rapidly, and we had never done so well financially.

Disappointed that I couldn't pursue my first love, I continued to paint, always feeling that people were looking down on me because I was dressed in painter's whites. I also found that most of the men I worked with were a little uncomfortable around me because I had developed large biceps due to lifting and moving ladders and five-gallon pails of paint. I was, as they say, "buff."

8

Married and Living in Hell

By the time we had completed the contract to paint the Simpson's downtown store, we had earned over $140,000, and, after covering our labour and material expenses, we were left with about $10,000. Having this amount of cash in hand, I decided to make one last pitch to Buzz by offering him the choice of going on a trip to Australia or getting married to me. Believe it or not, he took time to deliberate over my offer, and, after giving it due consideration, he replied, "Well, I guess we'll get married." At the time, my mindset was such that I never caught the fact that this man, who said he loved me, had to take time to decide if he wanted to marry me or not. We had been together for eight years, but Buzz had always taken the stance that a marriage certificate was only a piece of paper and nothing more. His other favourite reason for us not getting married was that we never had the money, only this time we did, so that argument wasn't relevant anymore. Now that we had the money, now that he had said yes, and now that the date had been set, we only had four months to get everything ready for the wedding.

Right from the start, I hit one roadblock after another and found out very quickly that getting married to Buzz wasn't going to be easy. The first thing I discovered was that he and his previous wife were not yet divorced and even though Buzz knew this, he displayed absolutely no sense of urgency and gave the impression that he just didn't care. Buzz was taking his usual relaxed approach to life, leaving me to deal with all the necessary paperwork, which I was quite prepared to do if only I could find what I was looking for. I immediately hit two major roadblocks when, after going through all of Buzz's personal papers, I was unable to find a copy of his birth certificate or his certificate of marriage. The situation went from bad to worse when I discovered that we would have to go all the way to Ottawa to get the necessary copies. By now, we were down to six weeks before our wedding, and I had no choice but to put pressure on Buzz to go to Ottawa to get the documents we required. Without them, we would not be able to apply for a marriage license. When Buzz finally got off his backside and made the trip to Ottawa, he was able to get everything that we required and all our paperwork issues were resolved. As expected, he had also left me to make all the other wedding arrangements and, with little or no thanks to him, we were finally married on 25th April 1987. The wedding went off without a hitch, and when I walked out of the church that day, I truly believed that things would change. Well, I must have been dreaming.

Having now reached the point where I had tired of painting, I decided to put my painting career behind me and find myself something different to do. I needed to find a job that would be a challenge, a job where I could use all of my skills and abilities, and so I made a decision to try my hand at selling real estate. After some research into what was involved, I signed up for the Real Estate course, and a few weeks later, in late August of 1987, I passed the exam and received my license to sell real estate. When a close family friend heard that I was now a licensed agent, he didn't hold back from telling me what he thought. He had no problem telling me to my face that I would never succeed in my new profession. Once again, I had been backed into that corner, the one that is reserved for those who will never succeed, who won't make it, and once again, I came out fighting. I was determined to prove our friend wrong. I was determined to prove the whole world wrong, so I went out looking for a broker who would take me on as an agent. I was very fortunate to find an opening with Robert Case Realty, where I was given the opportunity to work on my own and prove that I could sell real estate. In my usual manner, I gave my new profession my all, and before I knew it, the deals were coming together, and it was just like I had been doing it all my life. It seemed as if I could do no wrong and between the months of September and December of that year, I earned over $25,000, and it just kept coming.

Now that I was not working directly with Buzz, now that I was an independent woman, I was, to some degree, in control of my own destiny. With the money rolling in, I began to live up to my income by going out and buying myself a brand-new wardrobe and a nice new silver Chrysler Fifth Avenue. When Buzz saw the purchases, I had been able to make, he quickly came to the realization of how well I was doing in my new profession. So much so that he decided that very day to get out of the painting business and train to become an agent like me. In retrospect, I believe that he must have thought that selling real estate was easy, especially if I could do it, and if I could do it, he could do it better. Buzz signed up for the course, and by February of 1988, he too had received his license and had joined me at Robert Case Realty. At that time, the real estate market was beginning to take off, and I was closing deals at a fever pitch, which meant that the money just kept rolling in. Since I was doing so well and Buzz was not, I felt a little guilty about driving around in my new Fifth Avenue, so I went out and bought him a matching vehicle in the hope that it would motivate him. While I was busy going from here to there and back, Buzz would show up at the office, where he would always do one of two things, flirt with girls or play on the computer. Even though he always appeared to be very busy, whether at the office or on the road driving around in his new car, he never did sell a lot of real estate.

Now that I was earning all kinds of money as a successful real estate agent, we decided it was time to sell our small bungalow in West Hill and move up into a larger home in Pickering. Just after we had purchased our small bungalow, the real estate market had boomed, and when we finally sold it for $224,000, we had made a staggering profit of $128,000. We immediately rolled it all into a new three thousand square foot home for which we paid the exorbitant sum of $299,000. We took possession of our new home in May of 1988, and, at that moment in time, with all the other good things that were happening, I couldn't help but believe that the move to Pickering was a good thing. On the positive side of things, my son Chris was doing very well in his new school, where his interest in track and field continued to grow. On the negative side, I couldn't spend enough time with him as I was now forced to work harder, which meant working longer hours.

It had become quite evident that Buzz was only playing at selling real estate as he wasn't really putting any effort into it and was certainly not doing much of anything. He might as well have been retired because I was left to generate the income to cover the two car payments, the two cell phones, a larger mortgage payment, plus all of our other expenses. I found out very quickly that geographical cures don't always work and came to the realization that the move that was supposed to make me happy just wasn't doing it for me. What happened next was almost surreal when, out of the blue, my mother began to talk to me about God. My initial thought was that she had lost it, and even if she hadn't, I wasn't very interested in hearing about God from this woman who had been so mean and miserable to me all of my life. My mother had walked in fear all her life, and having done so, she was able to easily identify that same fear in me.

Knowing all the pressure I was under and the moments of overwhelming fear that I was dealing with, she told me that I needed to pray for the blood of Jesus over and around me. A day or so later, when I was amid one of these fearful moments, I remembered what she had said. I did exactly what she told me to do, and it worked. Immediately the fear left me, and peace came over me, instead of panicking, I was able to deal with the pressure and resolve the issue I was confronted with. As Buzz continued to enjoy the benefits of my success, he also became increasingly angry and upset at the long hours I was putting in at work. Since he had all day to kill, he had all day to feel sorry for himself and had convinced himself that his wife was neglecting him. The fact was Buzz no longer had the same control over me that he once had, and, as for me, I was so busy being a hotshot real estate agent that I didn't have a lot of time for him anymore.

Having made the move from West Hill to Pickering, we were now completely moved into our new home, where we were about to discover that everything was not as lovely as it appeared. When we first moved in, everything appeared to be normal but after a few days, we became aware of many things that were happening that we could not explain. It began one night when we were sitting down at the dinner table when during the meal Buzz felt someone touch his shoulder. Naturally, he turned around to see who was there and was quite taken aback when he discovered that there was no one behind him at all. Me being the skeptic that I was, I just laughed it off and really didn't pay too much attention to what had happened. Later that night, after putting Chris to bed, we were downstairs when we heard a loud bang coming from the upstairs level of the house. For the first time I sensed that something was terribly wrong in this house and a deep sense of foreboding came over me. I sent Buzz upstairs right away to see what had happened and when he came back down, he told me that he had found one of Chris' stuffed animals on the floor and presumed that we had heard it fall off the bed. I gave him that "Are you crazy" look that only wives can give and suggested that if a stuffed animal had made that loud thump, then it obviously had a rock in its belly. He just laughed at me, obviously thinking that this was all a big joke, a big joke that would soon be on him.

That night after going to bed, it seemed like I had just fallen asleep when I was abruptly awakened by something hitting me on the top of my head. I immediately rolled over and looked to my right and saw that Buzz was facing in the other direction, which meant that it could not have been him. Not quite able to figure out what had hit me, I settled my head back down on my pillow, and that's when I began to hear fingernails scratching on the sheet under my pillow. I was terrified, so terrified that I just laid there in the dark, not moving, not saying a word. Then I did the only thing that worked when I was afraid as a little girl. I pulled the covers up around my ears, leaving only my eyes and nose uncovered. It was only after doing this that a sudden peace washed over me, and thank God, I was finally able to fall asleep. When I awoke the next morning, I immediately told Buzz what had happened during the night. This time the joke was on him because, after hearing my story, he wasn't laughing anymore.

I headed off to work earlier than usual that morning, and as I was having my morning coffee at the office, I happened to share my experience of the previous night with a fellow agent. My co-worker appeared to be very knowledgeable about occurrences of this nature, and she surprised me when she suggested that we have a séance to find out what was really going on. As I relived all the events of the previous night in my mind, I was overcome with fear, and my response to having a séance was a definite, "No!" Not really wanting to go home that night, wanting to stay out of the house as long as possible, Buzz and I went out for dinner accompanied by our friend Helen. Helen picked us up and drove us to the restaurant, where we had a nice dinner, after which Helen dropped us off at home. As she was leaving, Helen was reversing her car out of the driveway back onto the street when she accidentally ran over Bennie, one of our three dogs. It was obvious that poor Bennie had been fatally injured and that he was in a lot of pain, leaving Buzz no option but to put him out of his misery. Before going to bed that night, Buzz and I locked up our two remaining dogs in the laundry room, which was where they usually spent the night. At around 4:00 am, we were both awakened out of a deep sleep when one of our dogs jumped up onto the bed. Realizing that the dog could not have gotten out of the laundry room unassisted, Buzz immediately got out of bed, put on his robe, and started to make his way downstairs to check things out. As I was lying awake in bed, waiting for him to return, I heard a crash and a thump, followed by loud moaning. I quickly jumped out of bed, put on my robe, and began to make my way downstairs, only to find Buzz in a crumpled heap about four or five steps down from the top of the spiral staircase.

Upon seeing him there, tangled up in the railing, my immediate thought was that he had suffered either a stroke or a heart attack which had caused him to slip and fall. Once again, that fear that haunted me flooded in and over me and gripped me tightly, so I turned around and yelled for Chris to get up and come and hold his dad while I called an ambulance. As I turned back to the stairs, you couldn't imagine the scare I got when I found Buzz standing upright right behind me. He was just standing there as white as a ghost, and for a moment, I thought that he was one. I helped Buzz back to bed and called an ambulance, and when the ambulance finally arrived, the paramedics came into the house, where they immediately checked his blood pressure. They found that his blood pressure was extremely low and, based on their findings, told me that he had probably just fainted while at the top of the stairs. While it seemed to be a reasonable explanation for what had happened, I couldn't help thinking how lucky he was to have only fallen four stairs. It had been a long twenty-four hours, and as much as I hoped that this was the end of the nightmare, little did I know that it was only going to get worse.

The next day my mother was scheduled to have some more cosmetic surgery. She had asked me to pick her up at the hospital as soon as she was released to go home. When I called the hospital at around 2:00 pm in the afternoon to confirm her release time, the nurse asked to hold for her doctor as he wanted to speak to me. After being on hold for what seemed to be forever, my mother's doctor came on the line and informed me that while she was in surgery, there had been some complications. I soon found out that this was somewhat of an understatement. He told me that my mother had suffered a massive coronary and that she was now on life support. I quickly got off the phone and called Buzz to have him come home so that we could both leave for the hospital as soon as possible. As we drove to the hospital, fear once again overwhelmed me as I began to relive all the memories that I had of my grandmother's death. I had watched my grandmother die a slow, lingering death, and, despite how my mother had treated me, I was inwardly terrified at the thought of seeing her totally incapacitated. Just when I thought that things couldn't get much worse, the front tire of the car picked up a nail and went very flat, very quickly. While Buzz hurriedly changed the tire, my mind was racing to and fro, wondering just what exactly was waiting for me at the hospital. After what seemed an eternity, the flat tire was removed, and the spare tire was installed, enabling us to get back on the road again.

Upon arriving at the hospital, we made our way to the ICU, where my mother was hooked up to a number of monitors and machines. I was so gripped with the fear of what I was seeing that my legs locked up, I could not move and. For almost an hour, I just stood there in the corridor outside of the ICU, unable to step in. It was only after the doctor came and spoke with me about my mother that I was able to slowly make my way to her bedside. I remember looking at all the wires and tubes that were coming from everywhere and wondering if she was going to pull through. No words can explain just how I felt standing at the side of my mother's bed. There I was, looking down at my mother, a woman who was always a going concern, seeing her lying flat on her back, fighting for her life. What made it more difficult for me was the fact that I was under the impression that it was my responsibility to tell her that she suffered a massive coronary. I had all these visions of her not taking it well and was extremely concerned that her reaction might bring on another heart attack. My concerns were all for nought because I later found out that the doctor had already informed her of her condition before we had arrived at the hospital. As I sat at her bedside, I watched her fade in and out of consciousness, fighting the breathing tube that had been placed down her throat. All I could do was tell her, "It's going to be okay. You need to rest now so you will get better." I spent several hours sitting with my mother until before I had to leave to pick up my son, Chris, from the sitter. After telling her that I would be back to see her the next day, I left.

After picking up Chris, Buzz dropped Chris and me off at home while he went to pick up milk at the corner store. When Chris and I walked through the front door, we immediately knew that something wasn't quite right since our dog Misty didn't come to meet us. Misty was a dog that always greeted us at the door, but this day, she was too busy keeping her eye on something at the top of the spiral staircase. She was sitting at the bottom of the staircase with her eyes fixed on something or someone at the top of the stairs, something or someone that we couldn't see. Once again, fear began to grip me, and my imagination began to run wild. What on earth could be holding her attention like this? Even though I tried several times to get her to respond to me, she wouldn't pay any attention to me at all and just kept looking up to the top of the stairs. Now almost in a state of panic, I grabbed Chris by the arm and ran with him into the family room, where I grabbed the phone and called Buzz on his car phone. Having managed to reach Buzz in his car, I blurted out that something was very wrong in the house and that he had to come home as fast as he could. After hanging up the phone, I sat Chris down on the couch and not knowing what else to do, I decided to arm myself. I made my way to the kitchen, where I got myself a big knife for protection. Since I didn't want to scare Chris, I brought along a tea towel with the knife, pretending that I was cleaning the knife with it. I was quite relieved when Buzz arrived home a few minutes later. Walking through the front door, he found the dog still sitting at the bottom of the stairs looking up to the top. Buzz immediately went upstairs and checked all the rooms to ensure that no one had broken in and found that no one was there. I must admit that I did heave a sigh of relief when he found nothing out of place. As for Buzz, well, he just laughed at me.

After the busy day that we had just gone through, the evening turned out to be just as hectic, and before I knew it, it was time to get Chris settled down for the night. While I was getting him ready for bed, the strangest thing happened. All the timepieces in the house stopped at the same time. A couple of hours later after I noticed that my wristwatch had started back up and, after checking the other clocks in the house, found that they had all started again at the same time as my watch. I was becoming more and more freaked out by all of these weird manifestations that were taking place in my home, and I had absolutely no idea how to address them. With all this stuff going on, the fear that I walked in caused me to get into the habit of checking every room, every closet and under every bed before I would go to bed. Eventually, because of my fear, I became afraid to enter any room on my own, especially after dark.

One night when I was checking up on Chris, I was going through my usual routine, standing at the door of his room and stretching up on my tiptoes so that I could see him without entering the room. Suddenly, he sat straight up in his bed with only the whites of his eyes showing. It was a scene I'll never forget, like the scene in The Exorcist when Linda Blair's head spun around, except this was not a movie. This was happening in my home. I was so scared that I literally leapt across the hallway into the adjacent room where Buzz just happened to be getting ready for bed. I was so gripped with fear that I was unable to catch my breath or to talk, and all I could do was point toward Chris' room. Seeing the distress I was in, Buzz quickly walked across the hall into Chris' room to check things out and returned a few minutes later to say that Chris was sleeping and that everything was fine. "What was the problem?" he asked. When I told him what I had seen, he looked at me as if I was crazy. I'm sure he thought I was losing my mind.

Just when I thought that things couldn't get much worse, the instant I walked through the door of my bedroom, I began to feel very sick. I was stricken with a severe headache and began to vomit. I not only looked deathly ill, but I also became deathly ill. It was an awful experience that I would not wish to repeat, and since there was no obvious reason for this happening and I didn't know what was causing it, I didn't know what to do to fix it. It was such a long night, and when it was finally over, I had only managed to sleep for a couple of hours. When I got up in the morning, even though I was tired, I was certainly feeling much better, and, as I had promised, I headed off to the hospital to see my mother. Although she was doing much better, she was still in the intensive care unit on life support because her oxygen levels were still too low. She was still unable to speak properly, the aftereffects of having a breathing tube down her throat. The only way she had of communicating was by writing, so she scribbled a short note on a piece of paper saying that she wanted to go home, that she didn't want to stay in the hospital any longer. It took some time to get through to her, but I managed to explain to her the seriousness of her condition and was able to convince her that it was in her best interest to stay where she was. After spending the whole day with my mother, I went home expecting to have a good night's rest, but I ended up with a repeat performance of the previous night. Once again, the instant I walked through my bedroom door, the headache and vomiting hit me and, whatever this thing was, it continued to affect me for the next nine days. The fact that this thing only happened when I entered my bedroom caused me to realize that there was more at play than the things of this world. When things finally came to a halt, I had suffered through nine days of hell and had dropped 15 pounds. While I never did find out exactly what was in my house, I am certain of one thing. It wasn't of God.

As the days passed, my mother's condition was improving by leaps and bounds. With her oxygen levels now elevated, she was taken off life support, moved out of intensive care and placed in a semi-private room. It was obvious to me that she was feeling much better and was on the road to recovery when she started back into her usual antics. My mother picked up where she left off before falling ill, making all kinds of demands. "Get me this," and "Get me that," and even though I did whatever she asked, it was never enough. She would call me from the hospital with a list of things she required, and I would stop whatever I was doing, put it all together and then head out for the hospital, which was in the west end of Toronto. After making the 40-minute drive, I would present my mother with everything she had requested, only to be told that whatever I had brought was not what she had asked for. Even when I sought out and bought the most expensive item, I was always told that it was never the right one or that it wasn't good enough. The harder I tried to make her happy, the more belligerent she became, and I was always left believing that, in her eyes, I was a complete and total failure. I finally got to the place where I had had enough of my mother going at me from one side and Buzz from the other, so I decided that it would be safer for both if I went back to work. I was desperately trying to hold onto my sanity and getting no help from either of them, so I figured if I was working, I wouldn't have to put up with any of their garbage.

Now that I was back to work, my contact with my mother was greatly reduced, along with exposure to her complaints, and the only complainer I had to put up with was Buzz. He constantly complained about our lack of money, having somehow missed the fact that I was the only one working and that he really needed to get off his backside, go to work and close some deals. Knowing Buzz the way I did, I knew that his selective hearing wouldn't receive that. However, despite his lack of effort, he did get his cheerful disposition back when I closed a few deals and the money started to come in. Because of the pressure that was on me to bring in the money, it became my sole focus, and I committed myself totally to that end. I worked very long hours, leaving home early and arriving home late. That way, I didn't see much of Buzz and saw even less of my mother. In a very short time, I became completely disinterested in my home life. I was more than happy to be at work. After all, it was the one place where I didn't have to listen to any complaints. Unfortunately, Buzz and I were on the financial merry-go-round, that vicious circle where having more money meant having more bills, and since I was the only one working, I was paying them all. When the end of the year came around, even though I was awarded a Sales Master's Award for my efforts, we were struggling financially. To celebrate receiving my award, at great expense, I booked us a room at the Sheraton Hotel in downtown Toronto where I also purchased tickets for the New Year's Eve party. I had a stinking, lousy, miserable time at that party, and when it was over, I knew something had to change in my life.

9

To Greener Pastures and Back

With all the New Year's festivities behind me, I was looking forward to a much better year than the one I had just gone through. I had ended the previous year knowing that some things had to change in my life, and, in retrospect, it was just as well that I had no idea just how much they would. During the latter part of the previous year, Danny, who was renting our basement apartment, had become my confidant during the difficult times I was working through with Buzz and my mother. For some months, Danny had been promoting my move to greener pastures by suggesting that if I left Buzz and went to live with him, life would be wonderful. Things at home went downhill so fast that, on the 11th of January, I sat Buzz down and informed him that we were finished. I told him exactly how I felt that I felt used, abused, manipulated, and taken for granted. I had had enough, and I wasn't going to take any more of his crap. Anxious to bring closure to our relationship and tie up all the loose ends, we put our house up for sale, planning to pay off all our debts and liabilities from the proceeds. While waiting for the house to sell, I went away for a weekend trip with Danny to the small rural community of Bridgenorth, which is located just outside of Peterborough.

While away from all the hustle and bustle of the city, I got completely lost in the peace and tranquility of the area. The atmosphere there was such a contrast to the chaos I was living in. It had such an effect on me that I decided right there and then to buy a lot and build in the area.

During the time that it took for the house to sell, even though I was a little fearful of Buzz, I continued to live in the home. When the house finally sold, it was a great relief to both Buzz and me, as we were both able to pay off all our debts and go our separate ways. With my share of the proceeds, which was around $50,000, I was able to go ahead with my plans to purchase a lot just outside of Ennismore and have a Viceroy pre-engineered home put up. While going through the construction phase Danny and I moved in together, and for the first time, I was able to see Danny as he really was. I found out very quickly that this man who had become my confidant and friend was not all that he had made himself out to be. He turned out to be a mean, evil, and nasty person. In all fairness to Buzz, he did try to warn me about Danny, but at the time, I was so hurt that I would not listen to anything he had to say. I was convinced that he was making it all up and was just saying whatever he had to keep me from leaving. I ignored the adage "that it takes one to know one," and the fact that Buzz was able to read Danny so well because he saw much of himself in Danny. As for me, if I had only realized that I was just burned out and that all I needed was a vacation, our marriage need not have broken up.

Since I had purchased a Viceroy pre-engineered home, every component was supplied pre-cut and ready for assembly. The manufacturer dropped two trailer loads of materials on the lot, and the local contractor I had hired assembled everything according to the drawings. It was quite amazing to see it all come together, taking only three months from the day I purchased the lot to the day when I could move into the completed home. At long last, I was able to make the big move to Ennismore, but instead of experiencing the peace and tranquility I had expected, I encountered the complete opposite. Instead of being happy there, I was miserable all the time. Nothing was working out as I had planned, and I hated everything about my life.

Now that I had made a move to Ennismore with Danny, I came face to face with the real Danny, who was none other than Mr. Evil himself. It was as if someone had flipped a switch, and the nice Danny, who had supported and comforted me, had been turned off, and in his place was this individual who would yell at me and push me around. He administered verbal and physical abuse, as I had never experienced before. It got so bad that I became extremely concerned for my safety, to the point that I asked my mother to move in with me. With each passing day, it became more and more evident to me that becoming involved with Danny was a terrible mistake. I wanted him out of my house, but because of his violent temper, I was terrified to tell him to leave. I left instead and stayed at my friend's house in Lindsay. When I returned to the house a week later to pick up some clothes, I was relieved to find Danny gone. I quickly had a locksmith come in and change all the locks to ensure that he would not have any further access to the home. I was fortunate that he never did return, and the concern that I had of him coming back to make a scene was never realized. With Danny out of the picture, I was now able to focus on the financial mess that was the aftermath of my involvement with him. I was left with a situation that offered me few options, and I was forced to claim personal bankruptcy to the tune of $275,000. I lost everything, including my house, my car, my boat, and my snowmobile. All that I was left with was my son and our clothes.

After dealing with the legalities of the bankruptcy, I moved from Ennismore to south Ajax, where I was able to find an affordable two-bedroom apartment for Chris and myself. The reality of my situation was now sinking in, the fact that in a matter of a few months, I had gone from basically having everything I ever wanted to literally have nothing. I was now relegated to living in an area where I didn't know too many people, in a low-rental apartment in which I had no furniture, no food, and little or no money. When Buzz heard the news about my split with Danny, the bankruptcy, and my subsequent move to Ajax, he decided to show up at my apartment door one day. As only he could, Buzz said all the right things, and, with me being as vulnerable as I was, we ended up sleeping together.

As the weeks passed, I continued to struggle in my new apartment, and just when I thought that my situation was as bad as it was going to get, I found out that I was pregnant. Next came the day that every parent prays they will never have to face, the day when their child goes hungry because their parent cannot meet the need. I had no food left in the apartment, and my son Chris was hungry. I didn't even have the fifty-four cents that I needed to buy a loaf of bread. As best I could, I explained to Chris that I didn't have any money left and told him to call his dad, thinking that since Buzz wasn't paying any child support, he might help us out. My little boy got on the phone and called his dad and, after telling him that he was hungry, asked him for money to buy a loaf of bread. His dad told him that he didn't have any money because his girlfriend had it all, and because she had it all, little Chris went hungry. Fortunately for both of us, I managed to get a job as a cashier at a Miracle Food Mart in Ajax. There I met a new friend who became my lifesaver over the next five months. It turned out that my new friend, Anne, lived in the same building as I did, and she took it upon herself to make sure that Chris and I were never hungry.

I found out through the grapevine that on the same day I announced to Buzz that I was leaving, he had gone to visit his old girlfriend, the one I had always been compared to and the one I had always been forced to compete with. She obviously still had feelings for him, and he for her because when Buzz and I separated, he immediately moved into her apartment. When the house in Pickering sold, and the proceeds split fifty-fifty, Buzz received $50,000, which he used for the deposit on a house that he and his girlfriend bought together. When he had learned I was in the family way, Buzz began to talk to me about reconciling, putting all the nonsense behind us, and starting over. Although it took a few weeks, he made the decision to leave his girlfriend, giving her his share of the house, and in June of 1990, he moved into my apartment. Even though Buzz had made a move to my apartment, he made it quite clear that he blamed me for everything that had happened, and, as far as he was concerned, it was all my doing. It was entirely my fault. Strangely enough, he considered himself totally blameless in the situation, and at no time did he ever accept or take any responsibility for the mess that we ended up in. It was obvious from Buzz's demeanor and attitude that he was angry at me, and when he didn't have anything good to say about me or to me, I couldn't help but wonder why he had even bothered to get back together with me. When I would say to him, "I love you," he would not respond to me in any way at all. When I asked him why he would not respond, he said, "I used to tell you that I loved you and yet you still left me."

It took some time for things to settle down and for the hurts to dissipate, and thankfully by the time my daughter Julia made her debut, things were about as normal as they were ever going to be. When Julia was born on the 8th of September 1990, she had a rough start due to complications I had experienced during my last week of pregnancy. Things were touch and go for a while, with us almost losing her in the first hours of her life. Thankfully, God had other plans. Now that I was a mother of two and had to meet the additional costs of having a new baby, I decided to venture back into the real estate business with the hope of earning some decent money. It didn't take me long to find out that my method of operation wasn't going to be like it once was. Having a baby at home changed everything. I was no longer able to work the hours I once did, and having to be home at a specific time had an impact on my ability to service my clients. Despite dealing with these new limitations, I continued to work very hard to put deals together, only to find them falling apart at the last minute. It seemed that the harder I worked, the worse it got, and it wasn't long before the lack of finances once again became an issue. Our financial situation eventually forced us to move into a house in Ajax, where we were able to rent out the basement to one of Buzz's friends. While all this was going on, our son Chris continued to excel in track and field, making us all proud when he won the Ontario title for running the fastest 100 meters in the twelve-thirteen age group. After moving into the house, Buzz had chosen not to look for work, and, with my lack of success in breaking back into real estate, it was just a matter of time before we ended up on welfare. I was very much relieved when Buzz finally stepped up to the plate, announcing that he and his friend had decided to go back into the painting business.

The next eighteen months just flew by, and my little Julia was growing by leaps and bounds, both physically and mentally. She was such a smart little girl, and it was absolutely amazing to see her in action as she demonstrated so many natural talents. To ensure that they were all properly developed, I decided to enroll her in Montessori, and this turned out to be one of the best decisions I have ever made. Often during the next eighteen months, I watched this little person put on a movie to watch, then immediately go to her bookcase and get the book to match the movie. She would then watch the movie and compare the text in the book to what she was seeing. This process enabled her to develop her reading abilities, and by the time she was three, she was already reading books. Shortly after Julia's third birthday, my father called from British Columbia to say that he and his wife, Libby, were flying to Greece on vacation and that they would be passing through Toronto. Since they were going to be on a layover for a few hours, Buzz and I picked them up at the airport and brought them to our home for a visit. While they were visiting with us, they were very impressed with my organizational abilities, particularly the way that I handled the children. When the visit was over, and we were driving them back to the airport, my father and Libby both suggested to me that I should use these abilities I had with children and open a daycare. While my initial response to their suggestion was to say, "You must be nuts," six months later, I was eating crow when I eventually took their advice and officially opened my first daycare. I had absolutely no idea that there was such a need for affordable daycare until I put an advertisement in the local newspaper and found the response to be quite overwhelming. Since I was operating my daycare out of my house, I took the living room and the dining room areas on the main floor and converted them into the main daycare area. I removed all my furniture from the area, and only those things that would be used by the children were allowed in that space. It took me about four weeks to get up to speed, and by the end of the first month, my daycare had grown to sixteen children, leaving me no choice but to hire a full-time person to help me.

Running a daycare turned out to be very hard work, as I now worked five days a week from five in the morning until six in the evening. To say the least, my schedule was grueling, and once again, I found myself repeating the pattern of throwing myself into my work with a passion to hide from my hurt and pain. To make matters worse, the woman I had hired to help me turned out to be quite forceful and very controlling, and I found myself having great difficulty dealing with her. Because of my life experiences, I still shied away from confrontation. I found myself taking too much direction and correction from her, leaving me feeling that I was the employee, not her. The interesting thing about this woman was that she was a Christian and had begun to talk to me about the Word of God. She got the same response that my mother had received when she started to preach to me, and that was, "I'm not interested."

At this particular point in my life, it seemed to me that the only people who wanted to talk to me about God were those who were making my life difficult. Perhaps, if I had seen some fruit in their lives, I might have been more receptive to what they were trying to share with me. A few weeks later, while the children were having their afternoon nap and we were having a cup of coffee, my employee began to talk to me about the "The Rapture." She explained to me how Jesus was going to return for His church, and that's when she said something that really caught my attention. She told me that if Julia and I were out in the car one day, and that was the day Jesus chose to return for His church, Julia would disappear, and I would be left alone in the car. Well, talk about getting my attention. The shock value of what she said gave me food for thought, and so began what can only be described as my slow conversion to Christianity.

As the weeks turned into months, I became increasingly exhausted, to the point that I found myself going to bed earlier and earlier, barely able to stay up past nine in the evening. On the one hand, I was now earning over $2000 a week, so money was no longer an issue, but on the other hand, my health was failing rapidly. Because my body was so overworked and my immune system severely weakened, when I caught a nasty virus, it quickly turned into pneumonia. I became very ill very quickly. I fought the symptoms on my own for over three weeks, not taking the time to go see a doctor. I finally became so sick that when my friend came to visit, she forced me to go to the Emergency at the local hospital. When the nurse took my temperature, it was one hundred and five point five, and before I knew it, I was hooked up to an intravenous drip that dispensed the antibiotics I required to make me better. Because of my condition, the doctor would not allow me to go home, and I was forced to remain in the hospital for the next five days.

While Buzz was able to bring both Chris and Julia to see me, he never once thought to bring me flowers or a "get well soon" card. As for my mother, she didn't come to see me at all while I was in the hospital, and she didn't even call me on the phone. Once again, it was hammered home to me that I was always expected to respond to the needs of Buzz and my mother, but when they should have responded to my needs, they never did. It's no wonder that I sometimes had a victim mentality, as I always felt that they took me for granted and never showed me any respect at all. I interpreted Buzz's lack of action as him sending me the message that he really didn't care about me, that I wasn't even worth the price of a Hallmark card. I viewed my mother's lack of response as just another confirmation that I was of no value and that I meant absolutely nothing to her. Once again, I found myself in that place where I had to deal with their garbage, which not only caused my stress level to rise but also brought back the fear. Oh, how I hated Buzz and my mother. Oh, how I hated my life!

10

Daycare Burnout

After my brief stay in the hospital, I returned home to pick up where I had left off since our financial needs did not allow me the luxury of taking a break from the daycare. From the moment I got home, Julia began to ask me to take her to church, and after two weeks of her pestering me, I finally broke down and promised I would. As promised, the next Sunday morning, we headed off to church, where I found the service both very interesting and very long. At the close of the service, the pastor gave an altar call, inviting all those who wanted to accept Jesus as their personal Saviour to come to the front of the church. I wasn't quite prepared for what happened next. My little five-year-old daughter, with no prompting from me or anyone else, made her way to the front to accept Jesus as her personal Saviour. I just couldn't get over the faith of this little five-year-old, particularly since I, as her parent, had struggled so hard with the whole concept of faith in God, primarily due to my life experiences.

The following Sunday, Julia and I were back in church, and once again, at the end of the service, the pastor gave the invitation. This time I sensed that there was a battle going on within me and. although it was only a matter of minutes, it seemed like an eternity passed as I struggled to make the decision of whether to go forward or not. When I finally came to the realization that all I had to do was believe, it just happened, and as I made my way to the front of the church, I actually felt the fear leave me. At that very moment, I recognized that I was a sinner and that my salvation came only through Jesus Christ. There was an instant shift. Julia and I continued to go to church regularly, and she would become completely lost in the praise and worship. She was totally uninhibited in her faith, and during praise and worship, she would think nothing of dancing before the Lord. Whenever the pastor would be praying over people who had come forward, Julia would go to the front of the church and lay her little hands on them, and begin to pray in agreement. Eventually, even Buzz came to the church, and after a short time, he also took a walk to the front of the church to meet Jesus. I must admit that I was suspicious of his motive, as the thought did go through my mind that he was only doing this to keep in step with Julia and me. My thinking was based on an emerging pattern of behavior that I was seeing, where Buzz would basically do everything that I was doing, almost as if he believed that it would please me or ensure the survival of our marriage.

While all of this was going on, my son Chris had chosen to go down another path, the wrong path, and it seemed that at every turn, he was getting into more serious situations. He had learned very well from his peers how to use the system, and the young offenders act was certainly not a deterrent to him or to any of the crowd he was hanging out with. They were all quite proficient at getting into trouble and equally proficient at manipulating the system when they were caught. As Chris continued to walk in rebellion, it was just a matter of time until he became a frequent visitor to several halfway houses for young offenders. I watched helplessly as he went from one bad situation to the next, and it got to the point that I began to feel that I was a failure as a mother. I allowed the results of his choices to distort my sense of self-worth, believing that if I had only done things differently, Chris wouldn't be the way he was. As usual, I was left to deal with Chris and his antics on my own as Buzz followed his usual pattern of not getting involved, which included him not giving me any moral support at all. Now that I was a Christian, I was expecting miraculous things to happen in my life and in the lives of my family members. But even though I was going to church every Sunday, I did not see the changes that I had expected or hoped for. So, to stimulate some change, I took my spiritual journey to the next level by being water baptized, this time by immersion, not sprinkling.

I continued to run my daycare, and there were many nights when, after my daycare children had all gone home, I would just sit down and cry. Not only was I stressed out over all my circumstances, but I was also stressed out over the expectations that I had placed upon myself to meet the needs of others. Moreover, the woman whom I had working for me in the daycare continued to be very controlling, which just added to my stress level, especially since I was not very good at handling confrontations.

What happened next was a series of events that finally brought me to the place where I was forced to deal with my employee face-to-face. It began with an incident one evening when Buzz arrived home from work, and Julia, seeing her daddy come through the front door, ran to meet him. In one smooth motion, my employee caught her by the arm, swung her around, and slapped her across the face as punishment for running into the house. None of the daycare children were ever treated this way, yet she treated my child this way. I was so fearful of that woman that I said and did absolutely nothing. As for Buzz, he stood there and waited for me to say or do something, and when I didn't, neither did he. On another occasion, when my son Chris went into the fridge to get himself a glass of milk, my employee told him to get out of the fridge, even though he was in his own home. It seemed that all my life, I had allowed or had been forced to allow people to cross my boundary lines.

It had always been that way, even when I was a little girl, but I now recognized that it had to change. I allowed this situation with my employee to go on for almost eighteen months until one morning. I reached my limit. She pushed me too far, and, just like Mount St. Helens, I blew. I had had enough, and when I told her to leave, she thought I meant for a day, not realizing that she was to leave and not come back. Now with my employee gone, I was left to take care of fourteen children by myself. Although I had to tough it out on my own for a few days, I took the time to decide what to do and where to go next. From time to time, over the next week, my former employee would call me just to say hello and to see how I was doing. I guess she was hoping to be invited back. At the close of our conversations, she would always leave me with a parting comment such as, "You know, you could fall down the stairs carrying those babies and there isn't anyone there you can call to help you." She just couldn't get it into her head that I was prepared to do it all on my own and that I could manage without her. After a week had passed, we finally talked over the situation at length and came to an agreement that she would take three of the children from my daycare. In effect, she would now have her own daycare in her own home, and this would provide her with the income that she needed.

When all was said and done, I felt that once again I had been taken advantage of, and, as usual, I took all the pain that

I felt and swept it under the rug. After the dust had settled, my life appeared to take a turn for the better, that is, until I got up one morning to find that my van was missing from the driveway. Despite being locked, it had been stolen during the night, and it would be over two weeks before the police would recover it and return it to me. The strange thing about having my van stolen right from under my nose was this, for the first time in my life, I felt violated. This event brought me to a place in my life where I believed that it was my lot in life to be the victim, that it was my destiny to be used and abused by everyone and anyone. Resigned to my lot in life, I just kept on going by pouring myself into my work and continuing to do daycare, where once again, the finances I brought in enabled us to get back into the housing market.

We were fortunate enough to find and buy another house in Ajax, one that was more suited in size and layout for the purposes of the daycare. When the time came to make a move into our new home and relocate the daycare, I was very fortunate to have all twelve of my daycare children move with me. Being able to keep all of the children meant that my income level remained the same, and I didn't have to advertise to find replacements. As time passed and the weeks became months, I once again began to exhibit all the typical signs of exhaustion and quickly came to the realization that I could not continue at this pace much longer. After some deliberation, I decided to make a call and ask my best friend, Anne, if she would like to come and work for me. What a relief when she agreed to join me, and knowing that she was more than capable of running the daycare, I was able to plan and look forward to a much-needed vacation. Planning around Buzz's schedule wasn't much of an issue as he wasn't working regularly as a painter. Since my daycare income was quite substantial, there was little or no pressure on him to work at all. As for Chris and Julia, going on vacation was a good thing, but being pulled out of school to go on vacation was even better. Although this vacation was supposed to be primarily for my benefit, it very quickly fell into the normal format of our vacations, meaning that it would be focused on the desires of others, which in this case would be those of Chris and Julia.

My son Chris had always wanted to try white water rafting, and, against my better judgment, I booked a rafting excursion down the Ottawa River. It was a wild ride from the start, and when I was finally ejected from the raft, I discovered that the water was both very wet and very cold. It was a terrifying experience for me, and I did not enjoy it at all. For the record, I swore that I would never do it again! After returning home from Ottawa, we quickly unpacked and repacked the van to get ready to leave for our second destination, Disney World, in Florida. A couple of weeks earlier, when my mother had learned of our vacation plans, she had conveniently invited herself and her boyfriend along on our trip. The premise was that we would all bond, and it would give us an opportunity to be a family, something we were not very good at. As usual, my mother didn't show up at the arranged time, and after keeping us waiting for an hour or so, she and her boyfriend finally showed up at the house. I immediately recognized him as one of her old beaus from when we used to live in Teesdale and, as the memories flooded back, I realized that he was one of the men in my mother's life who had tried to have his way with me when I was only twelve. I stifled all the emotions that were stirring up inside me and never said anything to him or to my mother because I was on vacation, and fighting and arguing were the last things I wanted to do.

Despite my efforts to maintain the peace, things just went downhill from the moment we left for Florida, and what was intended to be a nice family vacation turned out to be a total nightmare. It began with my son Chris choosing to argue with me about everything and anything. If I said something was white, he would say that it was black, and when the ensuing argument heated up, he would yell and curse at me, and I would respond back to him in like manner. The constant arguing and fighting took its toll, and instead of having a busy but enjoyable vacation, I was stressed to my eyeballs. While all of this was going on, Buzz took his usual stance, which was to say nothing and do nothing. When things got so bad that he was forced to respond, he would always take Chris' side in the argument. Instead of correcting his son for his lousy attitude, bad manners, and foul language, he was venting toward his mother, Buzz would find some reason to excuse Chris and correct me instead. Since I was the one driving the van to and from Florida, I was held hostage by the situation, having nowhere to run and hide. Even when we were in Florida, there was no escape from the verbal garbage that came out of Chris' mouth, and he just kept going on and on, knowing full well that there wasn't much I could do about it. In all my life, I have never been happier to return home from a vacation than I was from this one. It was by far the worst vacation that I have ever been on, and I swore that I would never do it again. Upon returning home, Chris' attitude towards me did not improve, and by the time he was seventeen, I had had enough of his nonsense. I finally reached the point where I told him to get out of the house and not come back. In no uncertain terms, I told him that I didn't want to put up with his bull or his rebellious spirit anymore and that since he was so unhappy at home, I was sure that he would be much happier out on his own.

All the stress from this family situation, combined with the long hours and the heavy workload of the daycare, eventually took its toll. Once again, I was completely exhausted and burned out, and in August of 1998, I closed the doors on my daycare for the last time, bringing to a conclusion yet another chapter in my life.

11

She's Just Like Me!

Now that my daycare was gone, the requirement we had for a large home was also gone, along with the large mortgage payment. Wisdom kicked in early this time, and after selling our home in Ajax, we were able to purchase an affordable modest home in Courtice. At the time, my major concern about the move to Courtice was how Julia was going to handle it. She surprised us both by quickly settling into her new school. It wasn't long before she was the premier paper delivery person in the neighborhood, having 196 customers. The move to Courtice provided me with a couple of things that I badly needed at this time in my life. It allowed me time to recover physically and also enabled me to experience a measure of peace and stability.

Shortly after the move, my friend Bud Ross suggested that I go through a program that was designed to help people deal with past hurts and issues. A week or so later, when I was presented with a 3" binder that contained a copy of the three-hundred-page manual that I would be required to study, my immediate response was to hand it right back. In retrospect, at that time in my life, my thought processes were very twisted and distorted. The fact that I declined the offer and sent the manual back was to be expected, as I had long since convinced myself that God could not love someone like me. I truly believed that I was a failure because I was always blamed for everything that had ever gone wrong. I truly believed that I was abused as a child because I was bad and not worthy of my mother's care and attention. I truly believed that I was used and abused as an adult because that was all I deserved.

I truly believed that I was a bad mother because of how my son had turned out.

I truly believed that I had to go along with what everyone else wanted because I didn't deserve to have an opinion.

I truly believed that I was of no value, of no consequence, and that I was totally worthless.

I truly believed that nobody cared about me, and I hated myself for being me.

My belief structure was such that I had become hardened because I was hurt, I was bitter, I was angry, and I had become so accustomed to being used and abused that I considered it normal. My anger and my pain showed with every word I spoke and with every move I made, but even though I was broken, I was still quite formidable and could be quite intimidating. Since that time, I have actually had people come to me and tell me that my attitude and body language used to scare them.

One evening while I was sitting in the family room of my home, something took place that enabled God to bring me a great revelation of who and what I had become. He used my daughter Julia to show me exactly how I acted and responded in a certain situation. As Julia was walking through the room, I made a comment to her, and when she answered me back, I was absolutely shocked at what she said and how she said it. It was as if someone had taken the blinders off my eyes and removed the earplugs from my ears. I was completely caught off guard, and when I finally realized what was happening, I remember saying out loud, "Oh God, No! She's just like me." Julia had become a mini-me, and this was obviously the last thing that I had ever wanted to happen. I didn't want her to be anything like me at all. I didn't want her to be used and abused like me. I only wanted the best for her. This incident shook me up so badly that my immediate response was to literally jump out of my chair and run for the telephone. When I finally found the phone, I called Bud Ross, the Christian Counselor who had originally given me a copy of the three-hundred-page manual. I quickly explained to him what had happened and told him that I was now ready to take the time to read the manual and go through the program. He was absolutely delighted that I had made the decision to go through the program, and he responded to me by saying, "Praise God, I have been praying for you."

When I got off the phone, I rushed out of the house, jumped into my van, and drove to Bud's home in Oshawa, where I was to pick up the manual. If anyone had told me a few months earlier that I would be making this trip to Oshawa, I would have said to them that they were missing it big time. After picking up the manual, I headed straight home, where I opened it up to page one and began a process that would, in time, set me free. Me being me meant that I threw myself wholeheartedly into the process of reading the manual, to the extent that it only took me six weeks to read through it, despite all of the interference I encountered at home. The interference began when I was about halfway through, with Buzz announcing that he had also decided to go through the program. My immediate response was to get quite angry with him as I knew full well that he was only going to do it because I was doing it. I remember thinking, "Here we go again. If Sharon does it, Buzz has to do it too."

I told Buzz right then and there that, in no uncertain terms, he was to touch me until I was finished with it, especially since I had certain places bookmarked for future reference. Needless to say, one day, when I was out of the house, Buzz being Buzz, having little or no respect toward my wishes, took out my manual to read some of it. When I came home, it didn't take me long to find out what he had done, as I quickly found that my bookmarks were no longer in the places where I had left them. I knew right away what he had done, and I was absolutely furious with him, believing that his actions were a deliberate attempt to rob me of my upcoming freedom. It was evident to me that Buzz just couldn't accept the fact that this program was what I needed to help me to get healed and that I wasn't doing it for him. I was doing it for me! It took me six weeks to read through the manual and complete several lengthy questionnaires, after which I was finally ready to go through the "Restoring the Foundations" program.

During this time, I had set up my small living room as a quiet room in the house, a place where I could spend time with God and just soak in His presence. Despite my efforts to keep this area special, it was often deliberately violated by Buzz in order to cause me upset and rob me of what little joy I had left. I persevered through the situation at home, and when I had completed filling out the last questionnaire, I called Bud to arrange a time and place to go through the program in early March of 1999. Bud explained to me that male-to-female or female-to-male counseling is not sound practice in the Christian realm, and it was necessary for us to have a female third-party present. Taking his sound advice to heart, I asked my friend Gail to accompany me to the sessions. Prior to going through the ministry sessions of the program, Bud had reviewed all my answers in the questionnaires I had completed. Many of the questions that were asked were very personal, and, to be honest with you, many of them were the kind that I would have preferred not to answer at all. However, I knew that it was necessary for me to answer them truthfully because I knew that if I didn't answer them that way, I might never find the freedom that I needed in my life. Knowing this didn't make it any easier for me to work through them with Bud and Gail. As we worked through them one at a time, I thought that we would never get to the end of them.

The ministry sessions began on a Monday morning and continued over a period of five days, with each session running approximately two and a half hours. I found out later that this ministry was called Theophostic, not that I had any idea what that meant at the time. All I knew was that I was hurt and broken and that I wanted to be healed once and for all. Just wanted to be whole. As the program unfolded, it caused me to journey back through the many areas in my life that had been deliberately hidden or forgotten because they were too painful or too difficult for me to deal with. Thankfully, God was with me every day, only allowing me to go through as much as I could handle at that time.

1 Corinthians 10:13

13: No temptation has overtaken you except what is common to mankind. And God is faithful; he will not let you be tempted beyond what you can bear. But when you are tempted, he will also provide a way out so that you can endure it.

As memory after memory began to flood back, I began to experience visions in which I was able to relive many of the situations that had happened in my past. One vision came where I was able to see myself as a little girl while my mother was holding both of my little hands on a hot stove burner, to punish me for something that I had done to upset her. I became greatly disturbed as I relived this situation all over again, and I remember thinking to myself, "How could God allow these things to happen to a little child?" I had no sooner thought it when I immediately saw a vision of Jesus holding my little hands under cold running water to soothe the pain away. I was immediately reminded of that scripture in Hebrews that says that he will never leave you or forsake you.

Hebrews 13:5

5: Keep your lives free from the love of money and be content with what you have because God has said, "Never will I leave you; never will I forsake you."

As my vision continued, the next thing that I saw was the huge oak tree that I used to sit on when I was a little girl living in London, Ontario. I was sitting there swinging my feet like I used to, only this time, I was not alone, as I could see that Jesus was sitting right next to me. As the ministry continued, God took me through many different areas of my life, through many of the most painful times I had lived through. God knew that I was now ready and able to face these situations, and, much to my amazement, in every situation, He showed me that I was never alone and that Jesus was always there with me. With day one of the ministry behind me, I headed home feeling quite drained, and as I drove, I wondered if this ministry was really going to make a change in my life. While my drive home was uneventful, when I finally arrived home, I came face to face with Satan himself. While I was standing in my kitchen waiting for the coffee to brew, I heard an audible voice speak, "You will never get free; you should just commit suicide." I was so startled that my initial response was to jump back, but as soon as I realized that it was the enemy talking to me, I stood on the authority that I have in Jesus. As a child of God, I told him that he had no authority over me, and I commanded him to leave in the name of Jesus. He literally left with his tail between his legs.

The next phase of the ministry was to take me through a session on forgiveness, where I forgave all the people who had ever caused me any hurt or pain. This was a lengthy process for me as I had to write down their names on a piece of paper, and then, after forgiving them for what they had done to me, I had to throw the paper in a garbage can. While it was very hard for me to forgive some of the people who had abused and misused me, I knew that if I was ever going to get free, I had no choice but to do it. It was after completing this exercise that Bud pointed out to me that there was one more person that I had to forgive. He continued by explaining to me the fact that I was still angry with God, blaming Him for allowing me to be used and abused all my life. Bud then told me to tell God how I felt about Him and, if I needed to yell at Him, I was to do just that. I can only imagine the look that I gave Bud. I am sure I looked at him as if he was crazy, and I said to him, "I can't yell at God!" He looked at me and calmly said, "Sharon, yes you can. You know that God understands where you are at, and doing this will allow you to complete the forgiveness process." As instructed, I did what he said, and even though I felt a little foolish, a little awkward, and even a little scared, I yelled at God and told him exactly how I felt. I must be honest and say that it didn't seem quite right for me, a mere mortal, to be telling the creator of the universe exactly what I thought of Him.

As day three began, we moved into the area of breaking off all the generational curses that had come down the family line, both from my father and from my mother. From there, we moved on to dealing with ungodly beliefs by taking the lies that

I believed about myself and replacing them with the truths of how God Himself sees me, changing them into Godly beliefs. As the ministry process progressed through the areas of hidden or forgotten memories, the forgiveness process, and the Godly and ungodly beliefs, I began to feel a peace come over me. Day by day, I was being set free from all the things that had held me back for so long, all the things that had held me captive and in bondage.

I now began to realize for the first time that, in spite of the circumstances I was in, in spite of the situations I was dealing with, God was in charge, and I was not. Each day of ministry brought me closer to the freedom that I had sought for so long, to the freedom that at one time I had never thought possible. The week just flew by, and before I knew it, it was Friday morning. I awoke with great anticipation of what might happen on my final day of ministry. Bud had me sit down in a chair, and then, after praying, he spoke directly to all the strongholds that had power over me. When he had finished, he and Gail prayed for me to receive a confirmation of the work done in me, and it was at that very instant that I received something I had not expected. As they were praying for me, God gave me a vision in which I saw a beautiful blue sky, trees, and a white dove. It was so vivid that my whole demeanor changed, and, seeing the change in me, they asked me to tell them exactly what I was seeing. As I shared with them what I had seen, Bud got quite excited and was beaming from ear to ear as he explained that the dove represented Holy Spirit and Purity. At last, I had received the freedom I had been searching for, and God had confirmed what I already knew, that I would never be the same again.

As I left Bud's home that day, he handed me a fifteen-page manual with instructions on how to use it over the next thirty days. It was a manual designed to help me walk out of the process. While it was one thing to be free, it was another to walk in the freedom that I now had. That afternoon I arrived back home as a brand-new person. I quickly became caught up in the Spirit and continued to praise the Lord into the early hours of the morning. To the best of my recollection, I spent most of that time on my face before the Lord. As for Buzz, well, he just watched what was going on and didn't say much. The truth is that he really wasn't quite sure how to handle the situation or how to handle me. As I prayed to God, I told Him to do whatever He had to do in me to make me the person He had called me to be and to make me ready to fulfill the plans and purposes He had set out for my life. Since that day, many different people have said to me that I pray dangerously. As far as I was concerned, I wasn't praying dangerously at all because I now knew that God was going to take all the hell I had been through in my life and cause it to be for good. I knew that all the experiences I had lived through had prepared me for the calling that God had placed on my life, even though I didn't know what it was yet.

12

Good Comes From Evil

While I am not sure at what time I eventually got into bed, I do know that I slept soundly through the balance of the night. When I finally awoke on Saturday morning, I got out of bed and got myself dressed. After making a fresh pot of coffee, I stepped out into the backyard to see what kind of day it was. It was an overwhelming experience for me as I looked around and saw the sky, the grass, the trees, the birds, and all of creation as I had never seen it before. It was as if I was looking through someone else's eyes; nothing was as it had been, everything had changed, and everything I looked at was beautiful. I soon realized that I was the one who had changed and that, for the first time in my life, I was seeing things as they truly were. It's amazing what you see when you are no longer seeing everything through a veil of pain, anger, bitterness, and unforgiveness. I sat down with my coffee and just took it all in, thanking God for what He had done to bring me freedom at last.

Later that same day, I received a phone call from Bud to ask me if I would like to accompany him and a few others who were going to the "Airport" that evening. "The Airport" was what everyone called the Toronto Airport Christian

Fellowship, the home of the "Toronto Blessing." I jumped at the opportunity to go to "The Airport" as it would allow me to praise the Lord and thank Him once again for what He had done for me. So, having accepted the invitation, I planned to pick up Bud at his home in Oshawa and drive him over to Pastor Bob's house in Ajax, where we were to meet the others who were going. Although I had attended the same church as Pastor Bob for some time, I really didn't know him very well at all, which caused me to feel a little awkward around him. When we finally arrived at Pastor Bob's house, he was standing outside patiently waiting for everyone to arrive. As I got out of my van and made my way up to the front door, Bud was already walking ahead of me and immediately asked Pastor Bob, "What do you think?" Pastor Bob took one look at me, and his response absolutely floored me when he said, "She's absolutely radiant. The Lord has done beautiful work in her." I was quite overwhelmed by his observation and his response, and it helped to put me more at ease in his company.

A few minutes later, the other ladies who were going with us finally arrived, and we all got seated in Pastor Bob's car to make the trip to Toronto. There was an air of excitement in the car as we headed toward the highway, with everyone talking and sharing what they hoped to see God do at the service that evening. After merging onto Highway 401, which would take us across the top of Toronto, what happened next was one of the most unusual spiritual manifestations that I have experienced to date. It began when Pastor Bob turned up the volume of the car stereo, and as the music played, a glorious warm anointing filled the car. Every one of us could sense the very presence of God right there with us, and as I sat in the back seat of the car, I became totally overwhelmed by the love of God. Then it happened. It was as if the car was driving through what could only be described as "waves of the anointing." As the car hit and passed through these invisible waves, all the others in the car would respond with a "Wow," "Oh," or "Ah." As for me, my reaction to this experience was that my whole body became like jelly, and I began to slide off of the seat onto the floor. Fortunately for me, I was sitting between two other ladies in the back seat of the car, and they were able to keep me on the seat and reasonably upright. Over the next 30 minutes, we must have driven through at least ten or twelve of these waves before we finally arrived in the parking lot at T.A.C.F.

I was so overcome by the presence of God that when it came time for me to get out of the back seat of the car, I couldn't. My legs were like rubber, and I had absolutely no physical strength or coordination to make things work. My companions literally had to pull and push me out of the car, and when they finally got me out, I had to be held up by Bud and Pastor Bob. With my legs like rubber, I couldn't lift my feet up, and I was dragging them most of the time, so they carried me across the parking lot and into the sanctuary. It was during this traverse of the parking lot that I lost my left shoe as it was dragged off my foot, and as hard as I tried, I just could not manage to get my toe back into that shoe. I was so affected by the presence of God that I was basically helpless, having little or no control over my physical body, having no strength and limited coordination, and barely able to talk. My friends were all laughing at my condition, and they took great delight in telling me that I was doing it all backward, that people usually got carried out of T.A.C.F., not carried in. There was a slight delay while one of the ladies retrieved my shoe and slipped it back onto my foot, after which Bud and Pastor Bob finally managed to get me into the sanctuary and seated on a chair. They sat me down at the end of a row, but when I started to lean too far to the one side, Pastor Bob suggested to the others that they move me into a couple of seats as he didn't want me falling off and blocking the aisle.

When the praise and worship began, I wanted so badly to stand up and give praise and thanks to God for everything He had done for me through the ministry I had received that week. I did manage to pull myself up onto my feet one time where, with the help of a chair back, I remained standing for about two minutes, after which I fell to the floor. It was impossible for me to fight gravity, so I spent the rest of that evening on the floor where Jesus Himself ministered to me. At the end of the evening, when the service and the ministry were over, Bud and Pastor Bob once again supported me as they helped me out of the sanctuary and across the parking lot to the car. I don't remember much about the drive back to Pastor Bob's house, as I was still very much affected by the presence of God that I was experiencing. At Pastor Bob's house, we had a time of prayer and fellowship, and as a group, we gave thanks to God for the miracle that He had done in my life. As the evening wore on, I began to realize that I wasn't in this thing alone, that God had placed me with a group of believers who would nurture and mentor me. For the first time in my life, I felt His peace, that peace that passes all understanding. That evening when I left Pastor Bob's house to go home, I was still totally engulfed by the presence and the love of God, and I now knew without any doubt that this was a new beginning for me. I was so saturated in His presence that I have very little recollection of dropping Bud off at his home in Oshawa and making my own way home to Courtice. What I do remember is that when I arrived home, I walked into the house to find Buzz all showered and smelling of cologne, having expectations of having sex with me, after what God had done for me that week after experiencing His presence as I had done that evening, having sex with Buzz was the furthest thing from my mind. Buzz was disappointed and quite unhappy when I told him that I had absolutely no interest in that area at that time.

During the previous five days of ministry and the Saturday evening spent at the "Airport," God had begun to reveal to me that much of what I had lived through was wrong. He had also begun to show me that many of my lifelong practices were also wrong and that there were areas in my life where things had to change. Not prepared to settle for anything less than a total commitment to the things of God, I chose to set my sights on Jesus and everything that He stood for. The result was that He became my all in all, with everything else becoming secondary. It was unfortunate that Buzz did not believe or could not accept that I had changed, that many things had changed. He continued as if it was business as usual, and it truly sickened me to know that his focus was on self-gratification and not on the things of God.

The following morning Sunday, after going through all the usual rituals, we all got into the van to drive to church. While driving to church, I decided to put on some praise and worship music, which affected me greatly as I was once again enveloped in the very presence of God. Once again, I found myself having great difficulty sitting up straight, and when we finally arrived at the church, I was barely able to stand up, let alone walk, when I stepped out of the truck. I was quite wobbly as I slowly made my way to the door of the church, and I am sure that some people thought that I was under the influence. Well, in a manner of speaking, I was under the influence of the influence of Holy Spirit, not the other spirits. As I walked through the door into the sanctuary, Pastor Bruce, who was our senior pastor, turned around and looked at me, immediately seeing the change in me. He took one long look at me and said it all when he said, "Wow! What a change."

Over the next two weeks, as I continued to seek the Lord daily, He enabled me to see for the first time how things really were in my home. He showed me that my husband had no respect for me, that he did not take care of me, that he had no love for me, and that I had been living a lie for almost twenty years. Having now committed my life to God, I asked Him to help me overcome these adversities and to help me become the person that He wanted me to be, not the person I thought I should be.

Over the next few months, time passed very quickly for me as I was growing in the Lord at every turn, and not a day went by that I did not learn something of value. Unfortunately, Buzz was not happy with my rate of growth, and it seemed that the more I grew, the more upset he became. To justify his actions, he would continually bring up my past and would get on my case by saying to me, "Well, you liked sex before. What's different now?" With every word that came out of his mouth, Buzz confirmed everything that God had shown me was wrong with my marital relationship. Like I said before, Buzz only saw me as being good for sex and work! He had absolutely no concept, no understanding at all of what had happened to me, and as often as I tried to explain it to him, he either could not or chose not to grasp it. I told him several times that there were certain sexual things I did not want him to do to me anymore, and his response was the same as it was when I was thirteen, when he said to me, "That's how I show love." As far as Buzz was concerned, it didn't matter what I said or what I wanted. If I said, "Don't do that!" he would go ahead and do it anyway, and when he was finished, I would often cry quietly while he would just roll over and go to sleep. This was a very difficult time for me, and I became greatly disturbed by what was happening to me. I told God that I could not understand why He was allowing this man to continue to abuse me, and I actually began to have difficulty acknowledging that God was in charge.

The group of people that I had gone to "The Airport" with would meet for prayer at Pastor Bob's house a couple of times a week. Since I had been given an open invitation to attend, I would go over occasionally when I felt the need for specific prayer, usually related to a desire for change in my situation. From time to time, I would be asked to pray for someone else who was there, but, despite doing my best, I always felt a little inadequate. The adage that "practice makes perfect" certainly applies to prayer, though, as the more often I prayed, the more comfortable I became. I eventually reached the place where I enjoyed the experience rather than only surviving it.

One night, as we all prayed together, the others in the group felt led to pray specifically for me, that I would receive the baptism in the Holy Spirit with the evidence of speaking in tongues. Even though I had heard all these people pray in tongues before, I didn't understand it well, and because I didn't understand it fully, I was very nervous about receiving it. Thankfully, they took their time with me and explained to me that this was a free gift from God, that it was available to me, and that all that I had to do was receive it. As I sat in the big comfy prayer chair, they laid hands on me and prayed over me, after which they commanded me to receive what God had for me. Initially, I was reluctant to speak out the words that I could hear in my spirit because I wasn't sure if it was just my imagination. At the right moment, Pastor Bob slapped me on the back and said, "Well, speak it out, woman. It's not just for you!" And that's exactly what I did. At that very moment, I spoke out in my new language, entering a new spiritual dimension for the first time, one of power. Now that I had been baptized in the Holy Spirit, I found myself being asked more frequently to pray for and minister to others. I also found that the more frequently I ministered to others, the more my own need for prayer diminished.

When we met together, it was not uncommon for us to have someone new show up, which resulted in the size of the group growing rapidly. A broad mix of men and women from various backgrounds would come to the meetings, and it always amazed me to see the wide scope of their needs. Ultimately, they all were there for one reason, that reason being that they required healing for one thing or another in their lives. As for me, my spiritual life continued to grow by leaps and bounds due to a combination of sound teaching and having an open heart for the things of God. As we as a group ministered together, I began to realize that God was now allowing me to see into the spirit realm. I had become a seer. A simple explanation of what a Seer is would be this: as I was ministering to a broken and hurting woman, God would show me exactly what had happened to her. The first time it happened to me, I was completely overwhelmed by emotion as I could see the abuse that the woman had endured all her life. In addition to seeing what she had experienced, I was also able to feel the pain she had inside her. It was quite horrific. It was also marvelous to see God move at these meetings, as there was never a night where someone wasn't healed, delivered, or set free.

As my participation in the group increased, I came to the realization that I was being trained in how to flow in the gifts that God had given me so that I might serve Him to the full. I could see how God was now using all the past hurts and pain that I had been set free from to enable me to minister healing to others who were where I once was. It truly is an awesome privilege to be used by God to bring healing to others and to be a vessel through which He flows. God basically took everything that was meant for evil in my life and turned it into good for others. I also understood that it never really was about me; it was all about the other hurting and broken people out there, those in this world that I would minister to in His name. I finally understood the reason I had been allowed to go through all the hurt and pain that I had endured. God had allowed it to happen so that I could minister healing and deliverance to others, as this was what He had called me to do so that I would bring glory to His name.

13

The Conference

As my journey continued, I truly believed that things were going to change for the better at home. Unfortunately, my hopes were short-lived when instead of things getting better, they actually got worse, much worse. Buzz knew me well, and he knew that when I had made the choice to make God number one in my life that I wasn't fooling around, that I was dead serious about it. I found that the closer I got to God, the more irritated and angrier he became with me, and he would show his anger in many different ways. Every time I would go out to a prayer meeting or to minister, he would give me a hard time when I got home, particularly if he wanted to have sex. If I said no, he would often force himself on me, and I would end up feeling violated. He got back onto his old kick of wanting me to wear sexy outfits to turn him on, and when I would say no to him, "I don't want to wear these things anymore," he would just ignore me and demand that I do what he wanted. No matter how often I spoke with him about what he was doing and how it was affecting me, he just totally ignored me. I just wasn't getting through to him at all, primarily because he wasn't interested in hearing what I was thinking or what I was saying. This was a very difficult time for me, and I had a hard fight on my hands to keep my eyes on Jesus. I was determined to become the person that God wanted me to be, and I had no intention of going back to where I had come from by falling back to my old ways.

Just when things were at their worst, a friend told me about a weeklong conference that was coming up at the "Toronto Airport", called "Releasers of Life". I felt very much in my spirit that I needed to be there, and I could feel the excitement building up inside of me as I made plans to attend. I was very fortunate when a couple of my women friends, Beverley and Gail, who were both part of the prayer group, agreed to come with me. Considering my situation at the time, the idea of spending a whole week in the presence of God really sat well with me, and Beverley and Gail agreed that it was the right thing for me to do. My decision to go certainly didn't impress Buzz at all, and he only agreed to my going when I stood my ground and made it perfectly clear that he didn't have any choice in the matter. With that settled, we three ladies booked the conference, along with a hotel room for the week, and impatiently waited for the day to arrive when we could finally set off for Toronto.

As the conference began, it was such a pleasure to be spending time with people of like mind, and we had so much fun together because we were all after the same thing, more of

God. At the conference, I sat under the ministry of Mary Audrey Raycroft and several other prominent speakers, all of whom spoke into my life and released the gifts that God had placed within me. I learned in one of the courses titled "Motivational Gifts" that even I had a place in the church. I learned that we are all one body, and if one piece is missing or not functioning properly, then the body isn't complete. At long last, I had received the revelation and the understanding that not only was I an important piece of the puzzle, but that I was a part of God's plan for His church.

Before we knew it, day three of the conference had come to an end, and with the evening service over, we reluctantly left the "Airport" and made our way back to our hotel. As usual, upon arriving back in our room, we reviewed and discussed all the happenings of the day and shared with each other what we, as individuals, had learned from the teachings. We weren't in our hotel room more than ten minutes when we received an unexpected phone call from Pastor Bob. When the phone rang, Beverley answered it and, when she had finished speaking with Pastor Bob, passed the phone over to me. I took the phone and listened as he began to speak, and it was immediately obvious from the tension in his voice that he was extremely upset. He proceeded to share with me what had happened to him that day and what he told me would change my life forever. Pastor Bob told me that he had received a phone call that morning from Pastor Bruce, asking him to come to his home to see him about an urgent matter.

So, at lunchtime that day, Pastor Bob had gone to Pastor Bruce's home, where Pastor Bruce came right out and asked him if there was anything going on between the two of us. Pastor Bob was both surprised and dismayed to be asked such a question, to have his integrity questioned, particularly since he was chasing after God, not after women, married or otherwise. He asked Pastor Bruce why he would ask him such a question, and Pastor Bruce told him that Buzz had come over to his home to see him the day before. While there, Buzz had told Pastor Bruce that things were not very good at home and that he suspected that his wife was having an affair with Pastor Bob. Upon hearing this, I immediately burst into tears, initially out of embarrassment but then out of sheer anger that Buzz would stoop to such a level in an effort to control me. When I got off the phone with Pastor Bob, I was so angry at Buzz for what he had done that if I could have gotten my hands on him at that moment, I would probably have killed him.

Having fully understood Buzz's motive for going to visit Pastor Bruce, I was furious at him for the lies and the slander that he was speaking out. Let's face it. He didn't want me going out to prayer meetings; he didn't want me going out to minister. He wanted me at home where he could control and manipulate me. Buzz had a plan, a plan that required him to create a situation that would cause me not to go out to the prayer meetings or to minister. By insinuating to Pastor Bruce that Pastor Bob and I were having an affair, he probably thought that would cause me so much embarrassment that I wouldn't dare show my face in church again. What made Buzz's claim so unbelievable and ineffective was the fact that we had a ministry policy in place that a man was not allowed to be alone with a member of the opposite sex or vice versa. In all the time that I had ever been in the company of Pastor Bob, we had never at any time been alone, as we had always been in the company of one other female. In retrospect, the one very prominent factor at play was that I wasn't having sex with Buzz the way I used to, and, considering Buzz's mindset and his priorities in life, he figured I was getting it elsewhere. It was becoming more and more obvious to me that Buzz did not want God to be number one in his life, and he was refusing to accept the fact that I did. It was also becoming more obvious to me that he was going to fight my choice all the way, and considering the stunt he had just pulled, it seemed that he would stop at nothing to change my mind.

I thank God for my two friends who were with me at the hotel as they were able to calm me down and convince me that there was no value in driving all the way home to Courtice to deal with Buzz. They helped me recognize that I was dealing with a direct attack from Satan and that my weapon of warfare against his actions was to pray against them. The next morning before the conference session started, I had an opportunity to speak with Mary Audrey Raycroft and was able to share with her what had happened the previous night. She was very supportive of me and listened to my story, after which she encouraged me not to be concerned or worried as God was in control, despite how things appeared. She then began to pray for me, and as she prayed, she had a vision in which she saw the Lord storing up treasures in heaven for me. I felt so much better after she prayed for me, and as I continued to seek God, I knew there was a change. It was a change that was much deeper than I had ever experienced before.

Before we knew it, day five of the conference was over and done with, and it was just after eight on Saturday evening when we headed for the highway to drive home. After dropping Beverley and Gail off, it was time for me to go home and face Buzz, and I remember being more than a little concerned about what I might be walking into. I guess that after spending so many years with Buzz, I should not have been shocked or surprised at what I found when I finally arrived home just after ten that night. I walked into the house to find Julia in bed sleeping and Buzz waiting for me, all showered and smelling of cologne, expecting to have his sex as usual. He didn't even ask me how my week had been at the conference, what had been taught, or what had happened during the ministry times. The only thing he wanted to do was get me into bed, and when I resisted, he began to become quite forceful, being determined to have his own way. I was already upset at what he had done earlier in the week, but now I was absolutely disgusted with him and with his silly perverted games.

With both hands on his chest, I pushed him back, moving him away from me, and asked him, "So, what did you do this week?" His response was very vague, as he gave me little pieces of this and that, nothing of any substance. Then I came right out and asked him, "Did you go to see Pastor Bruce this week?" He responded, "No, why?" With his response, Buzz confirmed to me at that very moment that I was now in a battle for my life. I then asked him, "Why are you lying to me?" He stood there with a straight face and replied, "I'm not." Then I told him every little detail of the phone call that I had received while I was at the hotel. I then asked Buzz to his face, "Did you say to Pastor Bruce that I was having an affair with Pastor Bob?" "No!" he snarled back.

At that very moment, I lost it. Anger and rage gripped me, and I said to him, "You're a filthy liar." Like a cornered animal, Buzz took the offensive and tried to intimidate me by getting right in my face. At that point, I told him in a very abrupt manner to "Back off!" I told him that I had warrior angels to protect me, and on hearing that, he really backed off and left me alone. He continued to claim that he had not made any contact with Pastor Bruce, to which I reminded him that the truth always comes out. I also told him that I wasn't playing games anymore and that I wasn't prepared to allow anything to come between me and God or to jeopardize my personal freedom or the ministry that God had called me to. I then left him standing there in the middle of the living room and went down into the family room, where I spent the night in prayer.

The following day, when I was speaking with the Lord, I asked Him why I was still here in this house and why I was still in this relationship. Then I told him that if He wanted me to stay where I was, I not only wanted Him to fix the mess, but I also needed Him to let me know what He wanted me to do. Even if it meant remaining in this excuse for a marriage, one in which I was being abused and misused, I just wanted to be totally in God's will. I also told God that if He didn't want me to be where I was, He was to show me clearly so that I wouldn't miss it, as I certainly did not want to venture out where I was not supposed to be. Little did I know at that time that this was exactly what He was about to do, so having prayed and believed that God would take care of business, I just stepped back and watched and waited. While I was waiting, I found out that when Buzz had accused Pastor Bob of having an affair with me, Pastor Bruce had told him that what he was saying could not be possible. He told Buzz that Pastor Bob was a man who had integrity, a single father who had put his own life on hold to raise his three children, two girls, and a boy. Pastor Bob was affectionately known as "Mr. Mom" by many of the congregation because he did all the things for his children that any mother would do, with few limitations. Pastor Bruce also told Buzz that he had accused the wrong person, particularly since he had been Pastor Bob's spiritual mentor for over 22 years. He also told Buzz that he knew the nature of the man, and what he was being accused of just wasn't in his nature. As for me, I was so concerned about what this accusation would do to Pastor Bob's reputation that every time we were at the same function, I made certain that we were always in the company of more than one person. After all, the Word says that we are to make sure that there is no appearance of evil, and I was determined to ensure that nobody would have the opportunity to speculate about anything.

I knew in my spirit that an amazing plan of God was about to unfold, and while I waited patiently to hear from Him, my birthday came around again. For the first time ever, Buzz went out and got me a birthday card and a birthday cake. After I got over the shock and surprise, I opened the card to read the text and found that Buzz had handwritten something inside. "Don't ever leave me." I couldn't help thinking to myself that the inside of a birthday card was not the place to write something like that, as it appeared to be more like an act of desperation than a card of best wishes. Buzz had finally realized that I meant business when it came to God and that I was not going to allow him or anyone else to control or manipulate me anymore.

14

The Apartment

I had often heard and used that age-old expression, "God works in mysterious ways," but what happened next took it to a new level for me. I was busy at work one day when I was paged to take a phone call, a phone call from a man I didn't know, a man I have since come to recognize as a messenger from God. When I took the call, the voice at the other end of the line asked me, "Are you looking for an apartment?" I immediately responded with, "Yes." He then told me that he had a beautiful two-bedroom apartment available in my building in Ajax and asked if I would be able to come and see it that afternoon. Again, I answered, "Yes," followed with my first and most important question, "How much is the rent?" Naturally, I was concerned about the rent amount as I only earned so much money, and I was obviously limited in what I could spend. His response to me was, "Don't worry about the rent. You will be able to afford it." After leaving work that day, I drove to Ajax to check out the apartment, and it was, as he said, beautiful, even having its own personal laundry suite. Considering how this had all come about, I felt that this was a sure sign from God, and, having now placed all my trust in Him, I made my way home to Courtice to tell Buzz.

As soon as I arrived home, I sat Buzz down and told him that I was leaving and explained to him how God had provided me with an apartment. I made sure to take my time and made sure I was very specific in my wording to him while reinforcing to him once again that God now came first in my life. Buzz now knew and accepted the fact that God was now number one in my life and that he couldn't argue with me about it, nor could he fight me for it. Later that evening, I sat down with Julia in my quiet room and did my best to explain to her why her father and I could no longer live together. Julia was a very intelligent little girl, and she had obviously known for some time that her father and I were not very happy together. She had been standing on the sidelines watching and waiting, being able to see and hear the fighting and arguing getting worse by the day. I made sure that she fully understood that she could see her dad anytime she wanted and that he was not going to be excluded from her life. She got quite upset and cried for a short time, and only after I assured her that everything would be okay that she accepted what was happening and became quite settled with it.

The next day, while I was on my break at work, I called Pastor Bob to share with him all the details of what had happened the previous day. Even though Pastor Bob had counseled and prayed with Buzz that the marriage situation would be healed and that there would be unity in the home, he wasn't surprised to hear that God had opened the door for me to leave. He agreed with me wholeheartedly that God was at work in the situation and that He was removing me from an environment that would destroy my spiritual walk. I then told Pastor Bob that God still had some work to do as it was impossible for me to rent a truck for the move because I didn't have a credit card. I also told him that this was only part of my problem, as I also needed someone to drive the truck for me because I had never driven a vehicle that large before. As my break was coming to an end, I had to cut the conversation short, but not before I asked Pastor Bob if he could help me in any way. He responded immediately by asking me, "When are you moving?" When I told him about the moving day, he said that he would book the truck rental, drive the truck, and also round up some help to move my things. Everything was happening so fast, everything was changing so quickly, and I had absolutely no idea at that time just how much my life was about to change.

During the week prior to my move, I was very fortunate to have my friend Beverley come over to my house and help me pack boxes and get all my stuff ready for the move. She was one of the ladies who was involved in the ministry group and was also a longtime friend of Pastor Bob's. Because of this, I felt very comfortable with her, and she had basically become one of my spiritual mentors. It was amazing to watch how God caused things to unfold as every little detail of my move came together in less than a week. Before I knew it, it was moving day. Beverley and I were busy moving boxes outside onto the driveway when Pastor Bob showed up at the house with the moving truck. He was accompanied by his son, Mike, whom he had commandeered to help. Buzz just stood back and watched the proceedings from the sideline, saying nothing as item by item, box by box, my half of the contents of the house were removed and placed in the truck. He was obviously not very comfortable with what was going on, and it seemed as if he didn't know what to do with himself while all of this was happening. While I felt no regret at all for leaving, what I did regret was that Buzz had chosen not to embrace God to the fullest, the way that I felt compelled to do. When I say this, I am not judging Buzz. I am basing it on the fact that he went through the same "Restoring the Foundations" program that I went through; the only difference was that he chose not to change.

With the truck finally loaded, Pastor Bob and his son, Mike, left for Ajax, with Beverley, Julia, and myself following behind them in my van. When we arrived at the apartment building, we were fortunate to have complete access to the service elevator, and the move went so well that my belongings were unloaded, and everything was moved upstairs into my apartment in record time. To expedite the return of the truck, everything was hurriedly moved into the apartment and not exactly put in its place yet, resulting in the apartment being quite a mess with boxes stacked everywhere. As Pastor Bob and his son left to return the truck, he stuck his head back in the door and said, "Get this mess cleaned up," then hurriedly made a quick exit before somebody threw something at him.

If I were to say that the first few weeks at the apartment were different, it would be quite an understatement. It was so totally different as all the stress, all the tension, all the upset, all the negative stuff that I was accustomed to dealing with on a daily basis were gone. Now that I was living in my own space, the atmosphere I found myself in was so peaceful that I was, at long last, able to focus on more positive things. I made a conscious decision that even with my work schedule, motherhood, and involvement in the ministry, I was going to do everything in my power to get closer to God. Part of this process was my desire to become more knowledgeable of God's Word, and this led me to enroll as a student at Rhema Correspondence Bible School. My initial reasoning for this was that I didn't know where God was taking me or what He had for me to do, so I felt I had to ensure that I had the necessary teaching. I also knew that it is written in the Word that I should study to show myself approved, and there was nothing I desired more than to have God's approval.

2 Timothy 2:15

15: Do your best to present yourself to God as one approved, a worker who does not need to be ashamed and who correctly handles the word of truth.

With my crazy work schedule, I was fortunate to have Pastor Bob's daughter, Amanda, as Julia's babysitter, especially since Julia's school was very close to their home. When I was scheduled to work the early shift, I was required to start work at 5:00 am, which meant that I would have to drop Julia off at Pastor Bob's house around 4:30 am. Rather than wake up the whole household, I was given a key to the house which allowed me to quietly bring Julia in and lay her down on the sofa, where she would go back to sleep until 7:30 am. As for Julia, she had not only adjusted very well to the separation, she had settled into our new routine much better than I had ever expected. We were also very fortunate that God had placed several loving people in our lives, especially sister Beverley, who was a great support to us and was always there for us in our time of need.

After a few months had passed, the time had finally come for Buzz and me to discuss our upcoming divorce, so I called him and arranged to meet him at the local coffee shop. Feeling a little anxious about the meeting, I deliberately arrived early at the coffee shop and, while I waited for Buzz to show up, went over everything in mind that I planned to say to him. It seemed as if I had been waiting forever, so when I checked to see what time it was, I found that Buzz was running true to form, late as usual. When he finally did arrive, he was all dressed up as if he was going out somewhere, and of course, he smelled of my favorite cologne. With the initial formalities out of the way, he went and got himself a coffee and sat down at the table in front of me. Wanting to get this meeting over and done with as quickly as possible, I got straight down to business. I spoke to Buzz about all the necessary paperwork that would be required before we could meet with the lawyer. In what appeared to be an attempt to minimize the seriousness of the meeting, he responded by saying, "Great! And here I thought that you had called me here because you wanted to frolic. But now that you have mentioned it, I was wondering if I would have to remain celibate for the rest of my life." I wasn't surprised by his response, and therefore I didn't react to it because the words he spoke merely confirmed the condition of his heart. When I look back at this whole episode, I truly believe that God removed Buzz from my life because he would have done everything in his power to destroy my walk. About a week later, we met with a divorce lawyer and completed and signed all the necessary paperwork that would bring yet another chapter in my life to a close. A few weeks later, I received a phone call from the lawyer to advise me that all the paperwork had been processed. He also reminded me that it would be a further thirty days for all the legalities to be finalized, legal, and proper.

What happened next was both amazing and overwhelming as God now began to bring women to me, women who were in the process of living through what I had lived through. I found myself ministering healing to these women, just as God had ministered to me, and I was seeing others delivered, just as I had been delivered. As I continued to minister with Pastor Bob and with Beverley, we became more like a family, and for the first time in my life, I was being recognized as an individual, not as an object. I truly loved the fact that God was now working through me to bring healing to others; it brought me a level of satisfaction that I had never experienced before. During our ministry sessions or prayer meetings, God now began to impart to Pastor Bob, Beverley, or to me visions of future ministry and events that were to come. In one of these visions, I saw myself operating in churches and auditoriums, ministering to abused and broken women. With all this revelation being imparted to me, I now had no doubt that God had a plan for my life and that He was about to take all that was meant for evil and make it for good.

Genesis 50:20

20: You intended to harm me, but God intended it for good to accomplish what is now being done, the saving of many lives.

15

God's Plan Comes Together

Now that I was settled in my own apartment, my lifestyle had changed so much from the way it was before. I was very busy at work, I was active in ministry, and I never seemed to have enough hours in the day. Before I knew it, Christmas was just around the corner, and I couldn't help but be a little anxious as this would be my first Christmas on my own. One evening, a week or so before Christmas, I received a phone call from Pastor Bob, who called to ask me if he could borrow my van the following evening. He explained to me that he had purchased a 26" television for a family member and that he had to pick it up at Sears in Oshawa. After picking up the television, he also had to transport it to Palmerston, which was about a two-hour drive to the northwest. Earlier that day, he had gone to pick up the television at the Sears loading dock, only to find that the box was too large to fit into the trunk of his car. Since the television was a gift for a family member, he really didn't want to take it out of the box, and even if he had, he wasn't sure if it would have fit through the door of his car. Pastor Bob's trip to Palmerston wasn't just to deliver a television; he was also taking his daughter Amanda and granddaughter Miranda with him as they were going to spend Christmas with the family there. I told Pastor Bob that he was more than welcome to use my van, and since my work schedule finished early the next day, I suggested that I pick up the television for him. That way, he would be able to leave earlier for Palmerston, not having to drive from Ajax to Oshawa and back.

When I finished work the next afternoon, I immediately went and picked up the television at Sears, after which I drove to his home with the intention of swapping vehicles with him for the evening. When I arrived at his house, I gave Amanda some help loading all of the Christmas gifts, along with her luggage, into the van. When we were done, the van was packed to the roof, leaving barely enough room for Amanda and little Miranda to sit in the center row of seats. With everything and everyone loaded, Pastor Bob was about to leave when he turned and asked me if I had anything special planned for that evening. When I told him that I was just going home to have a quiet night, he asked me if I would like to come to Palmerston for the drive. He told me that he would welcome my company on the way back as it was a long boring drive along a very dark two-lane country road. Since Julia wasn't home that night, I was going to be spending the night alone, so I accepted the invitation, and, with Pastor Bob at the wheel, we all left for Palmerston.

As we drove, the weather turned quite nasty, and having to deal with the wind blowing the snow and the icy road conditions, it took us almost two and a half hours to reach our destination. Upon arriving in Palmerston, we quickly dropped off Amanda and little Miranda and unloaded the television and all the Christmas gifts for the family there. Since the weather was getting worse, we didn't spend any time socializing but got back on the road as quickly as possible to avoid being caught in drifting snow on the country roads. Thankfully, the trip back turned out to be quite uneventful, and, despite the bad weather and the wintry road conditions, we arrived back at Pastor Bob's home in Ajax in one piece.

During the drive back from Palmerston, Pastor Bob and I talked about many spiritual things, including future ministry opportunities for me. Being the person I am, I had no difficulty asking Pastor Bob directly, "Are you quite certain that I will be involved in your healing ministry?" Without any hesitation, he answered, "Without a doubt." After this exchange, I remained pretty quiet for the balance of the trip home, probably because my mind was going a mile a minute. I had so much to think about, so much going on in my head, so many questions, and so few answers. Where was God taking me now?

Being the week before Christmas, I was kept very busy at my job with customers buying gifts for their friends and family.

Before I knew it, it was Christmas morning, and Julia and I got out of bed to spend our first Christmas together in our new apartment. Since it was her first Christmas away from her dad, I thought it was the right thing for me to invite Buzz over to spend Christmas day with her. While it was a little awkward for Buzz and me, we both knew that it was important for Julia, so we were very civil to one another. All in all, Julia had a good day with both of us and after eating Christmas dinner with us, Buzz finally left to go home to his own apartment. Julia and I living in our own apartment felt quite different, and, to be honest, even though I knew that it was the right thing, at times, it felt a little strange. Later that evening, after Julia was in bed, I remember sitting on my sofa, going over in my mind all the things that had happened over the past six months. Now that Christmas was over for another year, and new year was coming up fast, I asked God out loud, "God! Where are you taking me from here?"

A couple of days before I had gone to Palmerston with Pastor Bob, our friend Beverley had traveled out of town to Sudbury, where she was spending Christmas with her two children. Not wanting to overstay her welcome at her children's homes, she planned to return a couple of days before New Year's Eve. I was busy minding my own business at home when Holy Spirit prompted me to give Beverley a call at her daughter's home and to offer to pick her up at Union Station on her return. Being obedient to Holy Spirit, I made the call to Sudbury, and when the person on the other end of the line picked up the phone, the voice said, "Hi Sharon." It was Beverley who had answered the phone, and when I got over my surprise, I asked her, "How did you know it was me?" She laughed and said, "No, there is no call display on this phone, but Holy Spirit did tell me that you were going to call, and yes, you can pick me up at Union Station on Thursday at 7:20 pm." At that, our conversation ended, and when I hung up and considered what had just happened, I was once again in complete awe of how God works.

Now that I had to be at the train station on Thursday, I realized that it had been several years since I had been downtown Toronto. Since I knew that the downtown area had changed considerably, I thought it wise to call Pastor Bob and have him advise me on which exit to take and where to park. Since he was quite familiar with the downtown area, I quickly found myself in information overload. It was one of those situations where you only catch about 50% of what is being said. It was at this point that I spoke up and suggested to Pastor Bob that he might consider accompanying me to pick up Beverley, as this would certainly be a lot less stressful for me. I was quite delighted when he agreed to join me as this meant that if Beverley's train was delayed for any reason, we could always talk about the things of God. As for me, picking up

Beverley was good, and talking about the things of God was good, making this a win-win situation all around.

When the day arrived for Beverley's return, I hurried home from work and, after grabbing a quick bite to eat, made my way over to Pastor Bob's house to pick him up. Since he knew exactly where we were going and how to get there, he asked me if I would like him to drive my van. I agreed, and after swapping seats, we finally set off for downtown Toronto. Our traveling time into the city passed very quickly as the traffic was moving very well, and the conversation was good. Before we knew it, we were parked in the lot at the Air Canada Centre, which was about two blocks away from Union Station. Since it was a brisk, cold night, when we got out of the van, we had to do some speed walking from the parking lot to the station. When we finally reached Union Station, we entered the concourse and looked around for the location of the Arrivals Board. Seeing the board in the distance, we made our way over to it and quickly scanned the board to check if Beverley's train was on time. We were pleased to find that the train information was on the board and that it was still on time, still scheduled to arrive at 7:20 pm on Track No.5. With the train due to arrive in only twenty minutes, we decided to make our way directly to the track and wait for her there.

Leaving the arrivals board, we followed the signs, walking up some stairs, then down some stairs, turning to the left, then to the right, and finally arriving at Track No.5. As we patiently waited on the platform for Beverley's arrival, over the next forty minutes we saw five trains come in, but no train from Sudbury, and no Beverley. By this time, we figured that something wasn't quite right, and with wisdom finally kicking in, we made our way back to the Arrivals Board to get an update. Sure enough, we found that the board had been updated, and it now showed that the train we were waiting for was not scheduled to arrive until 11:20 pm that evening. When we approached the service desk and enquired as to the cause of the delay, we were told that heavy snow had delayed the train along the stretch of track from North Bay to Sudbury. By now, it was about 8:20 pm, and I turned and said to Pastor Bob, "What are we going to do for the next three hours?" He just looked at me and smiled, "I guess we can go and get a cup of coffee and sit and talk, or we can pray."

We left the warmth of the station and quickly walked the two blocks back to the parking lot where we had parked my van. Since we had approximately three hours to wait before the train would arrive from Sudbury, Pastor Bob said that he knew of a Tim Horton's coffee shop that was located a few blocks north. Once again, as we were driving, the conversation was primarily about where we saw the ministry going, who would be involved, and to what degree. Then the conversation took another twist as I was prompted by Holy Spirit to ask Pastor Bob this question, "Is that all there is, or is there more?" He turned and smiled at me, and then he said, "Yes, there is more." At this point, I just sat back quietly in my seat, listening to the music as we drove to the coffee shop, where we parked and picked up two coffees to go. While we were sitting in the van drinking our coffees, my mind was going flat out, and I found myself blurting out yet another question. I said, "The more you are talking about, is that between you and me?" Again, Pastor Bob just smiled and said, "Yes."

At that very moment, an ominous feeling came over me, and I actually became quite fearful for having asked him such a question. My friend Beverley had told me that in the past, other women who had been pursuing Pastor Bob had asked similar questions and had been completely shut down by him. While their motive had been to get into a relationship with him, mine was not, which was evident by my being obedient to Holy Spirit, and only asking what the Spirit was leading me to ask. While I certainly did not want to be stepping out of God's will or appear to be walking in the flesh, Holy Spirit was so heavy on me that I had no choice but to ask. My concern was all for naught because I later found out that three months prior to our conversation, Holy Spirit had spoken to Pastor Bob and told him that He was bringing us together to further the Kingdom of God. He had never mentioned this to anyone as he had been patiently waiting for a confirmation, and my asking the question was the confirmation that he was waiting for.

Having finished drinking our coffee, we made our way back downtown to the train station, only this time, we sat very quietly as we drove. I may not have been saying much, but my mind was running in overdrive, and I can remember thinking to myself, "Oh my goodness, how could this be?" I knew that we had a strong spiritual connection, one so powerful that when we ministered and prayed for people, the anointing would be overwhelming. On many occasions, the individuals that we ministered to would comment on just how much they sensed the presence of the Holy Spirit. When we ministered together, we complimented each other; what I would think, he would speak, and what I saw in the Spirit, he would know. What it really came down to was this, God requires willing vessels to do His work, and we were both willing.

As we were driving back to the train station, Pastor Bob told me that many years ago, he had been given a prophetic word in which God told him that He was going to bring him a wife. He told me that he had held onto that promise for a long time, having waited for fourteen years for the one that God wanted him to have. He smiled again, and then he said, "You know that God's timing is perfect." For the second time that evening, we arrived back downtown, parked the van in the same parking lot, and made our way to the train station. We agreed that we should not say anything of our conversation to Beverley and that we would wait for Holy Spirit to tell us when the timing was right for us to speak with her. Having made our way to Track #5 again, we didn't have long to wait until Beverley's train finally made it in from Sudbury, arriving at 11:30 pm. When Beverley finally emerged from the train and stepped onto the platform, she was so happy and relieved to see that we were still waiting for her. Rather than carry Beverley's luggage all the way to the van, Pastor Bob went to get the van from the parking lot while Beverley and I caught up with all that had happened to her in Sudbury. About ten minutes later, Pastor Bob arrived outside the main entrance to the station to pick us up, and after loading the luggage, we headed for the highway. The driving time to Whitby passed very quickly, with the three of us talking, and after dropping Beverley off at her apartment and Pastor Bob at his house, I drove myself home to have a serious talk with God.

Pastor Bob had invited Beverley and me over to his home for supper on New Year's Eve, where we were going to sample his renowned crock-pot chicken. I arrived shortly before Beverley and found him still busy in the kitchen, working away in his usual manner with his trademark tea towel thrown over his shoulder. He was still preparing the food for our meal when he stopped what he was doing, turned quietly, and asked me, "Could I have a hug?" I said, "Yes," and that's exactly what I got; I got a hug. As he released his hold on me, he turned back to the counter and continued preparing the food for our meal. Then he asked me, "So! What do you think, Sharon, is this of God?" Without any hesitation, I answered, "Yes, I do believe so." He continued, "You know, Sharon, that nothing can happen between us until we are married." I felt like I was a schoolgirl all over again as I experienced the emotions of feeling excited, scared, giddy, and silly all at once. Not wanting to misunderstand or read anything incorrectly into what was being said, I asked him, "Could you be a little more explicit in what you are saying?" He turned to me and said, "I do believe that God has ordained this relationship, that it is His will that you and I become one. I would like you to become my wife and lead a God-like life with me while we minister healing to God's people." Wow! What a mouthful.

Thank goodness there was a sofa right behind me, as I was able to sit down on it before I fell over. Seeing my condition, he poured me a cup of tea and brought it over to me, placing it on the coffee table in front of me. He then sat down in his easy chair and, while looking me straight in the eye, asked that all-important question, "Will you?" I looked at him in utter amazement, and there was a short pause that seemed like an eternity while I inwardly asked myself if I could actually fill the role of a Pastor's wife. Then the realization came to me that if this was what God wanted, then God would have to equip me to handle everything that a Pastor's wife must deal with. As far as I was concerned, God was going to get what he wanted, and I looked at Pastor Bob and said, "Yes." He smiled at me and asked, "Can I have another hug?" I, of course, said yes, and while we embraced each other, we were both quietly wondering where God was taking us from here.

Looking at the clock, Bob said to me that Beverley would be arriving soon and that we should not say anything to her unless we got the okay from Holy Spirit. As expected, a few minutes later, Beverley finally arrived, and after a brief time of fellowship, we all sat down to a lovely dinner. All through the meal, Beverley was looking at both of us as if she was waiting for us to tell her something. At last, Bob said to me, "Okay, Sharon, go for it." Knowing that it was now okay for me to tell Beverley everything that was going on, I said to her, "You are not going to believe what I am going to tell you." "Yes, I will," she said, "God has already told me what is going on. The day you called me in Sudbury, He told me that you two were getting together and that I would be part of the ministry." So much for our big surprise! We were upstaged by God, who had confirmed what He had brought about by telling Beverley everything that was coming together. Through our being brought together and working through all the circumstances and events leading up to it, we both learned some very valuable lessons. The main one was that we both came to the knowledge that when God brings something together, He will always confirm it, either through His word or through another person.

With the New Year celebrations over, we all looked forward to a new season in the Lord, and what a season it was going to be. A few days later, I took the time to sit down and have a long talk with Julia. I asked her what her thoughts were if I were to marry Pastor Bob. I was absolutely floored when she replied, "Great, Mom. I kind of knew this was going to happen, especially with all the dreams I've been having." Up to this moment in time, I had absolutely no idea that Julia walked in the prophetic and that she had a prophetic calling in her life, just like mine.

16

The Wedding and More

Now that God's plan was coming together, Bob and I had to go through the process of informing all our family and friends that we were making plans to get married. It was quite a disappointment for us when we encountered some serious resistance from some of Bob's immediate family members. What was even more of a shock to us was the fact that they had absolutely no difficulty making it perfectly clear how they felt about our intentions. In spite of their resistance, our plans progressed, and within the next two weeks, the date was set, and all of the arrangements were made. Since neither of us had a large family or circle of friends, I had asked Bob's daughter, Amanda, to stand up for me, and he had asked his son, Mike, to stand up for him. My daughter, Julia, was absolutely delighted when she was asked to be a flower girl, as was Kyla, Bob's youngest daughter.

Having decided that we would honeymoon in Niagara Falls, we arranged for one of Bob's friends, who was the pastor of a church there, to perform our marriage ceremony in his church. And so it was that on April 14th, 2000, before a small company of twelve family and friends, we were finally brought together in marriage. After the ceremony was over and the photographer was finished taking pictures, we all drove back to the hotel where we were staying and had dinner in the hotel restaurant. When the meal and all the formalities were over, our guests left to return home, leaving us to spend our honeymoon in Niagara Falls.

We had a great time just doing all the usual tourist things, like going down to see the falls, doing some shopping, going out on the Maid of the Mist, dining out in the local restaurants, and basically spending quality time together while getting to know each other. The honeymoon was over in a flash, and after spending a couple of days in Niagara Falls, we returned home to Ajax on Sunday afternoon to begin our new life together. Over the next few days, we systematically moved all my belongings out of my apartment and into Bob's townhouse. Then came the difficult task of going through everything we had and making the required adjustments that must be made when two households come together. As difficult as it was, I was so looking forward to making a fresh start, especially since this one had God's blessing.

Prior to getting married, Bob and I had left the church we had been part of and had begun to attend Christian Life Centre, a P.A.O.C. affiliate. Our move had been driven primarily by the fact that Buzz continued to attend services at our old church, and this was causing some of the congregation there some discomfort. The situation was further complicated by his "poor me" demeanor, with which he was milking the situation for all it was worth. He certainly had the ears of some of the people in the church and, with the story he was telling, was receiving all the sympathy and attention he could handle. At that time, it did not seem appropriate for Bob or myself to disclose the truth behind my divorce from Buzz, so we opted to let God deal with him without any help from us.

Now that the wedding was behind us, we were still somewhat dismayed that some of our children were not very happy about our marriage. At the time of our marriage, Bob's son was 27, and his daughters were 24, 20, and 9, while my son was 19 and my daughter was 9. The one having the most difficulty with our marriage was Bob's oldest daughter, Alyssa, who was 24 years old at the time. Not only was she having great difficulty accepting me as her father's new wife, but she also just couldn't seem to accept my daughter, Julia, as her stepsister. Her response to Julia really caused me considerable upset because Julia had been so excited about becoming part of a big family. She had been looking forward to having another big brother and three big sisters, and she was quite distraught and unable to understand why Alyssa did not accept her. I soon learned a very valuable lesson, that when you are dealing with the trials and tribulations that life brings, you can fight it, or you can take the opportunity to learn from the experience. Initially, I did it the way I had always done, by fighting it all the way. Then I got smart and backed off and allowed God to do what He had to do. We went through some difficult times during those first weeks and months, and on more than one occasion, I found myself asking God if He had made the right decision by bringing us together.

When Kathy, a mutual friend of ours, learned of our marriage, she called our home one evening to extend her congratulations. During her phone call, she took the opportunity to remind us of the prophetic word that Bob had been given back in 1996, a word that contained some information relating to the wife that God had for him. Over the years, while Bob had held onto the promise given in the word, he had obviously pushed the details to the side. Now that Kathy had brought it up, she took the opportunity to remind him. In the word, God had told Bob that He was going to bring him a wife that would come alongside him, but she would be more than a wife. God said that she would be a helpmate that would pray for him, minister with him, and she would walk in all the gifts of the Spirit. God also told Bob that he was not to decorate the new house that he had just bought, that he was to leave it for his wife to decorate. God further told him that his wife was a gift from God and that she was being given to him to take care of, and that he must remember that she was fragile.

Since Bob always saved any prophetic word given to him, he immediately pulled up his personal prophecy file on his computer, and there it was, all of it. Every single detail that was in that prophecy covered everything that I did for Bob, even down to the decorating of the house, which was really easy for me as I had been an interior decorator for a number of years. Even the word fragile that had been used in Bob's prophecy was the correct word to use, particularly if you were describing my condition at that time. Despite having gone through the "Restoring the Foundations" program, I wasn't 100% healed yet, and even I did not realize just how fragile I still was. Now that I was married to a Pastor, a man of God, it didn't mean that my life was going to be easy and that everything was going to be perfect. I actually discovered the reverse to be the case, and I found that more and more, I was turning to God for the answers that I needed and not relying on my own understanding.

When I got married to Bob, I had no idea at the time that, over the next 18 months, my life was going to be turned upside down and inside out. I had no idea of the many lessons that God would teach me and just how much the enemy, Satan, would use the people I loved to try and destroy me. As Bob and I became quite active in our new church, we found that the presence and power of God had increased dramatically in our lives. As we continued to minister together, we found that

God had begun to open some doors of opportunity for us to minister to the broken, hurting, depressed, and oppressed people that He brought our way. I was now able to see firsthand how the ministry that I had gone through had set me free and healed me from many of the things that these people were going through. As I ministered to these people, I could see how God was taking all the evil that I had endured and causing good to come from it. Just as things were breaking forth in the ministry, the enemy moved in and used Alyssa, Bob's 24-year-old daughter, to bring all kinds of trouble and wreak total havoc in our family. It was an awful time, and things got so bad that I began to question why God had brought Bob and me together because I surely didn't need or want any more of this kind of garbage.

Before I had come onto the scene, before Bob and I had been brought together, he had become quite comfortable living on his own. Just like me, he was self-sufficient, used to taking care of everything himself, including the cooking, cleaning, laundry, full-time work, ministry, and still doing all kinds of things for his kids. Even after we were married, his children would bring any clothing that required repair over to our house because Bob also did all the sewing. This created a real dilemma for Julia and me, as we had great difficulty trying to fit into a family where it seemed that one half didn't want us and the other half didn't need us. It seemed to me that everything I did wasn't quite up to anybody's expectations, and if Bob did speak to me about something that I had said or done, I would usually get upset and end up in tears. Even though I tried very hard and made every effort to develop a relationship with Alyssa, I wasn't successful at all, probably because for any relationship to work, it requires effort from both parties. On the other hand, I got along famously with Amanda, Bob's 20-year-old, probably because we were alike and had much more in common. My relationship with Amanda was also influenced by the very special attachment I had formed with her daughter, Miranda, whom I just loved to pieces. There were many times when Amanda was a great help to me, being able to explain to me from her perspective the complex nature of her father's relationship with Alyssa. On several occasions, Bob had suggested to me that the best way to deal with Alyssa was to avoid confrontation, not to get in her face, but to be gentle and quiet. I tried dealing with her that way for a while, but when I saw that it wasn't working, I knew that the time was rapidly coming when I would have to take a more direct approach.

My opportunity to clear the air came quite unexpectedly one day when Alyssa called me to tell me that she really needed her living room painted. In the course of the conversation, she asked me if I would be able to do it for her, and I immediately responded by saying that I would be quite glad to paint her living room. I told her that I would go over to her house the next afternoon with my color charts and that I would help her select the right color to complement her furnishings. As promised, the next afternoon, I helped Alyssa pick the color most suited to her furnishings, after which I went and picked up the paint and began to paint her living room. I took full advantage of having Alyssa alone and having her undivided attention. I was able to tell her exactly how I felt and how much I hated how she continued to treat both Julia and me. I made it perfectly clear to her that she had no right to treat us the way she did and that I would no longer allow her or anyone else to abuse us or walk over us. I honestly believed that I would see some change, but when the change that I expected did not happen, I could only assume that my words had fallen on deaf ears.

What happened next was not good because when I saw that it was business as usual, I stopped trying to be accepted by everyone. I gave up trying and told Bob that we were in serious trouble, that we had reached the point in our marriage where we needed some counsel. What we needed was some outside advice on how to handle these family issues because we were both too close to them and were not in agreement on how to handle them. We were fortunate enough to know a couple of excellent Christian counselors, Bryan and Linda, who lived in Barrie, both of whom had been associated with Bob for a number of years. Knowing that it was expedient for us to resolve some, if not all, of these issues, we called them to see if they were home and if they would be available to meet with us. Upon hearing a summary of the situation, they immediately told us to come and see them that day, so Bob and I drove up to Barrie with the realization that our marriage was in jeopardy.

I thank God for competent Christian counselors, especially ones who speak the truth whether we want to hear it or not. When we met with Bryan and Linda, they basically told us that Alyssa had been allowed so much latitude that it had allowed her to affect what was happening in our home and in our lives. Because of past practices between her and her dad prior to me coming along, she had been allowed to create for us what could only be described as a nightmare. If Alyssa had a financial need for whatever reason, she would always phone and ask for some assistance and would always receive what she asked for. The fact that her father now had a wife who also contributed to the finances didn't mean anything to her, and she in no way made any effort to acknowledge that fact. Alyssa did not recognize that it was only proper that her dad would consult with me first before saying yes or no to any of her requests. She basically got anything that she asked for, and even though it came from my contributions to the home, I received no acknowledgment from her. I was left believing that in her eyes, I was a non-person and that even though she would take my money or my time, she had absolutely no respect for Julia or me. While there was no excuse for her behavior, Alyssa really didn't know any different, as this was the way she had always been allowed to operate.

When Bob and I left Barrie that day, we left with an abundance of fresh revelation and insight on how to deal with the problems that we were experiencing. As we talked about the situation during our drive home, Bob told me that he would take care of the issues related to Alyssa and that he did, even though she was not too happy about what was said. As they say, "Push had come to shove," and although we would have preferred another option when it came to shove, we were right up there with the best. With our new boundaries now in place, the situation with Alyssa now took a bit of a twist when her daughter Jessica became a pawn in the game. Unfortunately for Alyssa and Jessica, Bob made the decision that we were not playing games, and this resulted in us not seeing Alyssa and Jessica for some months. On the flip side, there was Bob's son, Mike, who was actually very happy that his dad was now married, and he even called me mom at times. After the dust had settled, for the first time in his life, Bob was finally happy doing the things that he wanted to do without the distraction of others.

As an onlooker, it was very easy for me to see that Bob had gotten into the habit of doing everything for his children and nothing for himself. Wow! Did we ever have a lot in common in this area? It was almost scary to see that he had done everything that I had done. In the past, we had both focused on taking care of all the needs and wants of our children and our spouses before taking care of our own. Our children and our spouses had always come first, regardless of what we needed, and Bob, just like me, would go out shopping and end up buying something for someone else and nothing for himself. Just like me, if he had needed an item of clothing and someone else declared a need or a want, his or her request would have been met first. My issues started way back when I was a child when, as the result of the treatment I had received, I was trained to believe that I did not deserve anything and that on any scale, I always came in last. And much like Bob, I had carried this belief and practice into my adult life. Because I had gone without as a child, I vowed as a young mother that I would never raise my children to be in lack. I had also made the commitment that I would do everything in my power to ensure that they would never grow up to think the way that I thought. In fulfilling my vow, like Bob, I had trained my children to have expectations to the point that it had become a detriment to us all. When God finally brought this revelation to me, it made it so easy for me to see why Bob's children were just like mine. It seemed that nothing was ever good enough for them and that the more we gave them, the more they wanted, the more they expected.

Now that God had cast some light on the situation, I was finding it much easier to handle all these problems, and it became even easier after Bob put his foot down. His children finally got the message, and they came to the realization that their dad was now living his life for himself and not for them. I finally became part of the family, accepted and not rejected as I had been all my life. In retrospect, I have to say that I believe this experience was part of God's plan and purpose. It was allowed to take place so we might learn these things before we continued on the path that He had set out before us.

17

Motivating to Ministry

Having just finished doing my housework, I sat down with the intention of taking a five-minute break when the phone rang. When I answered the phone, I was quite delighted to hear the voice on the other end of the line; it was Pastor Ruth from the church. She was a beautiful woman of God who was the Pastor of the Women's Ministries at the church. She was calling to invite Bob and me to meet with her to discuss some ministry opportunities that she had opened at the church. After a lengthy conversation with her, I made an appointment for us to meet with her one week later at her office in Christian Life Centre. At the appointed day and time, we met as arranged, and it was obvious from the start that she was very interested to hear where we had come from and where we saw our ministry going. After asking us all the usual pertinent questions, we spent the balance of our time with her discussing the importance of teaching the body of Christ, the church.

During our discussions, I happened to mention a seminar that I had taken while attending the "Releasers of Life Conference" at the T.A.C.F. The seminar was titled "Motivational Gifts" and had been presented by the founder of "Releasers of Life", Mary Audrey Raycroft. I explained to

Pastor Ruth how I had learned so much by attending that seminar, primarily because it had brought me to the full understanding that God had a plan and a purpose for my life. In addition to this most important revelation, I had also been made aware of my motivational gifts and how and where these gifts fit into the body of Christ. Pastor Ruth then asked me if I still had the material that was handed out at the seminar, to which I replied I was sure that I still had it somewhere at home. I told her that I would do my best to find it for her so that she could prepare a teaching on the "Motivational Gifts" and present it to the ladies of the congregation. She just looked at me and laughed, obviously knowing something that I didn't, and then she dropped the bombshell when she said, "I'm not doing it, Sharon. I want you to do it." With a lump in my throat brought on by fear, I still managed to blurt out, "Forget it. I can't teach. Are you crazy?" Pastor Ruth then said to me, "Yes, you can. You are gifted that way. You teach by your own experiences." "No way," I responded. "I'm too shy." "We'll see about that," she said. There was absolutely no talking her out of it. She had made her mind up, and as far as she was concerned, I was going to teach the seminar. As we left Pastor Ruth's office that day, my mind was running in overdrive as I attempted to grasp what had just happened.

Ever since Bob and I had begun attending Christian Life Centre, I took every opportunity presented to me to promote him and not me; this was part of my master plan. Now that God had gotten Himself involved in this situation, the complete reverse had happened, and the whole thing had been dropped in my lap. As Bob and I left the church that day, I was, to say the least, a tad overwhelmed by what I was facing. As we were driving home, the conversation continued between us, with Bob repeatedly saying to me, "Yes, you can teach, Sharon. I have watched you minister to others for over two years, and I know that you can do this." I just couldn't figure out why this was all happening. After all, I had gone to that meeting to promote my husband, and I had left that meeting knowing that God was now in the business of promoting me. Bob reminded me of that biblical law called the "Law of Reciprocity." In simpler terms, you reap what you sow. Upon arriving home, I made my way to our office, where I searched for, found, and pulled out all of the materials I had been given when I attended the "Motivational Gifts" seminar. I handed it all over to Bob so that he could read it through and give me his opinion on the material. While he was reading the material, my mind was just racing as I was still not convinced that I was capable of teaching any seminar to anyone. When Bob had finished reading, he turned to me with a quiet air of confidence and said, "Let's go and prepare a teaching."

Since the basis of my teaching was material compiled by Mary Audrey Raycroft, the first thing I did the next morning was contact her at the T.A.C.F. to obtain her permission to use some of her materials. When I spoke with her, her response was phenomenal. Not only was she delighted with what we were doing, but she also offered to send us a copy of all the base material that she had used to prepare her seminar. When I told her how I had been roped into this situation and that I was very nervous about the whole thing, she encouraged me by saying that she had been teaching for over ten years and that she still got nervous. When I got off the phone with her, I remember thinking to myself, if Mary Audrey Raycroft still gets nervous, what chance do I have? Since that conversation with her, I have had the opportunity to speak with a number of other teachers and have been able to enquire how they feel when they begin to teach. I now have it from a number of reliable sources that when you reach the point where you are no longer nervous, then you are in control, and God is not. As for me, I'd rather have God in control. I'd rather be nervous!

Thankfully, Mary Audrey was true to her word, and within a few days, I received a large package in the mail. It contained a full copy of all her original notes, all her source materials, and of course, all the information we would need to put our package together. Bob and I also went to our local Christian bookstore, where we purchased a couple of other books on motivational gifts with which to supplement our materials. At last, we were ready, and with more material than we knew what to do with, we began to prepare our own "Motivational Gifts" seminar, one with our personal touch and perspective. Over the next three months, we painstakingly worked through all the materials that we had, spending countless hours writing and rewriting the presentation material. Piece by piece, it all came together, and, at last, all the overheads, charts, graphs, and handouts had been finalized. When we had finished putting the complete package together, I delivered the large binder with a set of overheads and handouts to Pastor Ruth for her to approve. The approval process involved Pastor Ruth going through the material with our Senior Pastor, who was a very busy man and very difficult to get an appointment with.

It took about a week for Pastor Ruth to get in to see the Senior Pastor, but after reviewing the seminar material with him, we received his blessing to go ahead and teach it. Immediately after her meeting with the Senior Pastor, Pastor Ruth called me at home to give me the good news and to make arrangements to come over to our house so that we could discuss what we should do next. We got together a few days later, and after a lengthy discussion, the decision was made to limit the offer of the seminar to the members of the church body at Christian Life Centre. Offering it to people that I knew, people that knew me would give me an opportunity to practice the presentation and to see what kind of response it would generate. By the following Sunday, we had an insert in the church bulletin, a slide in the PowerPoint presentation, and several posters on various doors throughout the church. Now that we had gone public with my first seminar scheduled to take place only six weeks down the road, you cannot imagine how nervous I became. I was so concerned about my ability to teach, so concerned that I would make a mistake or say something wrong or not be able to answer a question someone asked, that I studied and studied, and studied, and studied some more.

The six weeks passed very quickly, and the day finally arrived when I was to teach the seminar. Even though I arrived at the church with a measure of fear and trepidation, I also had the certainty that God was with me. After all, He was the one who had set me up! At the appointed hour when we were scheduled to begin, Pastor Ruth opened in prayer, after which she introduced me to the participants. I stood up to begin to address my first group. With my knees shaking and my voice quivering a little, I said, "Good Morning." When I opened my mouth, the fear and trepidation disappeared, and the words just flowed. Before I knew it, it was four hours later, and I had just finished teaching my first seminar on "Motivational Gifts." Many of the people who had taken the seminar made a point of coming to speak to me later, thanking me for having shown them that they too, have a place and purpose in the body of Christ. The truth is that all of us have an ordained destiny that

God has placed within us, and that includes even you, the reader. What it really comes down to is this, "Are you, as an individual, prepared to choose to step out of your comfort zones?"

With my first seminar over, Pastor Ruth and I stepped aside to go through all the test sheets that were handed in by the participants in order that we might determine what ministry they were best suited for. One by one, we compared the individual results to the ministry opportunities that were available in Christian Life Centre at that time. Next, we presented these results and opportunities to the group, and of the twenty participants, twelve stepped out of their comfort zones right into ministry. Over the next few months, it was so gratifying for me to see them working in the areas of ministry that they had been called to. All they needed was to be shown where their motivational gifts lay, to be encouraged to step out, and to be given the opportunity to do so. Pastor Ruth was so enthusiastic about the results of the seminar that she immediately scheduled another one for two months down the road, with this one focused on the ladies who attended the Ladies Bible Study. When the time came for me to present the seminar to the Ladies Bible Study group, even though I was still a bit nervous, it was nothing like it was the first time. The experience and the confidence that I gained through my first presentation made it easier for me to move out of my comfort zone. Once again, the response from the participants was phenomenal, and I saw much fruit come from my teaching, as many more people were released into various ministries within the body at Christian Life Centre.

The success of my "Motivational Gifts" seminar now began to open doors for me, and more and more opportunities were made available to me, not just in the area of teaching but in the area of service. Shortly after my first seminar Pastor Ruth had recruited me to become the communion coordinator, which involved setting up the teams to cover the various sections of the church. The communion servers were also responsible for performing the altar ministry after communion, and it was such a privilege to pray for the needs of the individuals in the congregation. Pastor Ruth also began to use Bob and me as a couple by having us make hospital visitations on behalf of the church. Recognizing my organizational skills, Pastor Dan asked me to become the coordinator for the summer Vacation Day Camp that catered to over 100 children every year. While I coordinated, Bob became the Vacation Day Camp fundraiser, and we quickly discovered that as we worked as a team, God blessed our efforts.

In early June of 2001, the Senior Pastor announced that the church was going to hold a special awards night. He explained that it was being held, first of all, to recognize the congregation as a whole and, secondly, to recognize eight individuals who had made a special contribution to the body at Christian Life Centre. As I sat there, I watched the various Pastors handing out awards to people that I had come to know and love. I was very happy for all of them because many of them had been around for years, and I could see what their efforts had accomplished. When our friend Pastor Dan stood up to make the next presentation, he started by saying, "This award is for a lady who has brought life to the church by teaching others that they have a place in it." I still hadn't caught on to what he was saying, even when he continued to say, "After preparing others for ministry within the church, if they didn't take a position, God help them, for she would just hunt them down. Her name is Sharon Holburn." As he spoke my name, I finally realized that he was talking about me, and realizing that God had chosen to honor me for my efforts, I was so overwhelmed that I just burst into tears. As I stood up and made my way to the front of the church, for the first time in my life, I knew that my Heavenly Father was happy with me. He was happy with what I was doing, happy that His people were being motivated into service, and all the praise, honor, and glory was going to Him. When I reached the front of the church, Pastor Dan presented me with a beautiful plaque that was inscribed as follows:

Sharon Holburn

Motivating To Ministry Award, 2000-2001

"to prepare God's people for works of service so that the body of Christ may be built up"

Ephesians 4:12 (NIV)

Having received this "Motivating to Ministry" award, I was filled with such mixed emotions. I was shocked, I was happy, I was shaking, and I was teary-eyed. I was completely and totally amazed at how everything had unfolded, that this would ever happen to me, especially when I was only doing what God had called me to do. It's true that part of me felt that I did not deserve to receive the award, but then I realized that God had caused me to be recognized and rewarded for my obedience and my faithfulness to Him. Knowing that my Heavenly Father cared for me so much that He rewarded me in this manner only encouraged me to go deeper into the things of God. While I continued to teach my seminar on the "Motivational Gifts", I expanded my repertoire to include teachings on "Anger", "Offence", and "The Jezebel Spirit", to name a few. In the months that followed, further ministry opportunities opened up to Bob and me as the church began to send us people who were in need of personal counseling, healing, and deliverance. Then the phone calls started to come from outside our home church. Pastors were calling us to come to their churches to teach their people and to minister healing and deliverance to all aspects of their lives. In early October of 2001, Bob was approached and asked if he would teach a course on the "Spiritual Gifts" as detailed in 1 Corinthians chapter 12. With the course prepared, it was scheduled to take place every Friday evening over a one-month period, but what was expected to last for four weeks was extended by Holy Spirit and ran for twelve weeks. It was almost as if God had selected everyone who attended because the ones who did attend were obviously true God Chasers, and it was easy to see that these individuals were seeking more. Led by Holy Spirit, we had the privilege of teaching this small group of believers for the next twenty-eight months. God is surely good!

18

Sickness in The Family

During all these good things that were going on, particularly in the area of ministry, my mother had experienced a series of mini-strokes. My mother, being the busy, active person that she was, never stopping for a moment, never slowing down, came through all of them without realizing that anything had even happened to her. Even I didn't even realize that anything was wrong with her until one day while talking on the phone with me, her speech became more and more slurred. Now you must keep in mind that the only time my mother ever called me was to complain about something or someone. She would never start a conversation with, "Hi, how are you?" She never said, "Hi, how are kids?" She would immediately break into a lengthy dialogue that concerned her and only her. Her phone calls to me were a continual barrage of negativity. "I can't this, I can't that, this person is using me, or that person is abusing me," and so on and on and on. I had actually come to that place where I was absolutely saturated with her negativity and her complaints, so much so that I just couldn't stomach the continual pity party that she was having. To be truthful, I really dreaded her phone calls and would often make excuses as to why I couldn't talk to her. Sometimes I would tell her a bare-faced lie and say that I was just on my way out and that I would call her later. My reluctance to talk to her didn't seem to slow her down at all, as she was just like the energizer bunny, going on and on and on, continuing down that same path that she had been on for years. If nothing else, my mother was consistent, and, as always, she was the center of her whole universe. It was all about her and about nobody else. As for me, I had reached the point in my life where some, if not most, of my mother's practices were beginning to annoy me intensely, and I was rapidly reaching my breaking point.

For example, at Christmas time, my mother wouldn't take the time to wrap any Christmas gifts that she was giving. She would just throw them in a plastic bag and present them that way. Birthdays were also a real treat for my children and me because that's when Nannie would normally give us something from her house that she didn't want anymore. Strangely enough, when she received a gift from us, her expectation was that whatever we gave her would be brand new. After all, she believed she was entitled to that. When I looked back at the various gifts that were given to us over the years, it was obvious that she didn't consider any of us to be of much value or entitled to anything at all. It would be true to say that for my mother, there was nothing personal about her gifts or the way in which they were packaged or delivered. What made matters worse was that my children saw what she did, and yet they said absolutely nothing to me about their nannie's actions. The situation with my children was further aggravated due to the fact that my mother never ever spent any time with Chris or Julia, and it was becoming more apparent that they both felt rejected, just like me. There was one occasion when my mother took a well-used doll that she had picked up at the Goodwill store, dressed it in some old baby clothes, threw it in a green garbage bag, and gave it to my daughter, Julia, for Christmas. When Julia saw what her nannie had done, she just said, "Thank you, Nannie," and put the doll on her bed. Later, after her nannie had left, she said to me, "Mom, I really don't want it, but I don't want to hurt nannie's feelings either." I told her that I understood how she felt and that if she didn't want to keep the doll, it was okay.

I just could not understand my mother's logic as she obviously wasn't hurting for cash since she always had hundreds of dollars in cash in her purse. She knew that the gifts that she received from us were always brand new, and I always made sure that they were beautifully wrapped with fancy bows and tags. No garbage bags for me. In retrospect, I probably did this to compensate for what she had never done for me as a child. The fact that she was doing the same thing to my family troubled me greatly. Every Christmas, my mother would comment on how well I had decorated my home, how beautiful my Christmas tree was, and how well I had wrapped all my gifts. Her annual disclaimer statement would follow where she would always say, "I don't have any time to do stuff like that." I have never understood how my mother could expect us to accept her claim that she didn't have the time as she was a retired single woman living on her own. She had a standard list of excuses as to why she was too busy. If she wasn't getting her nails done, she was getting her hair done. Or she had to go shopping for clothes or groceries. And let's not forget that she had to go dancing. It was the same old garbage. Always the same old excuses, and frankly, they were wearing very thin, to the point where I was ready to blow.

By August of 2001, my mother's health had deteriorated dramatically, so much so that she now had the appearance of being ill. By this time, her speech had become so slurred that you couldn't help but notice it, and there were times when it was almost impossible to understand what she was trying to say. One day I plucked up all my courage, and I asked her point blank if she realized that her speech was becoming so slurred. She was quite surprised, almost stunned, that I had asked the question, and after a brief pause, she looked at me and said, "I think I've had a mini-stroke." She then admitted to me that about six months before, she had experienced some difficulty moving her hand but that the symptoms were temporary and had quickly disappeared. I suggested to her that she should see her doctor and get checked out right away because the fact that her speech was so slurred was not a good sign. Thankfully she took my advice and went to see her doctor, who immediately referred her to a specialist. Lab tests confirmed that she had indeed suffered not one but a series of mini-strokes. My mother's solution to the specialist's diagnosis was to increase her intake of the vitamin pills that she had been taking for years, believing that they would maintain the status quo. Ever since I was a child, she had always carried with her a container full of pills; all mixed up, none of them identified because she didn't have time to sort them out. Unfortunately, her solution was a temporary one because a short time later, she started to have difficulty swallowing and experienced a few tense moments when she would start to choke. Despite her deteriorating health, my mother was quite determined not to allow her condition to interfere with her day-to-day activities; absolutely nothing was going to stop her from going dancing.

One memorable Saturday afternoon, Bob and I had invited all the kids over to our house for a family barbeque. While I was busy cleaning up some things the in the kitchen, I heard the phone ring, so I asked Amanda to answer it and take a message for me. It turned out to be my mother, and I heard Amanda say to her, "I'm sorry, Sharon can't take your call right now." My mother then said to Amanda, "I can't breathe," and hung up the phone. When Amanda came back into the kitchen and relayed her message to me, and then told me that the line had gone dead, I immediately suspected the worst. I dropped what I was doing to phone her back but when I called her number the phone just rang and rang at the other end. Since she wasn't picking up her phone and it had only been a minute or two at most since she had hung up, I immediately presumed that something serious had happened, that she had possibly collapsed. After telling Bob what had happened, I began to panic. After pulling myself together, I called 911 to request that an ambulance be dispatched to her apartment. Bob and I ran out of the house and jumped into our van, breaking all the speed limits, along with a few laws, while racing to my mother's apartment in Oshawa. I was so worried and upset that I cried all the way there. As we arrived at her apartment building, we saw that the ambulance was just pulling out of the driveway. I jumped out of the van and flagged it down to inquire if they had my mother on board. The driver and his partner were not very happy when they told us that she wasn't at home, and they didn't know where she had gone. As the ambulance left, Bob and I buzzed the apartment superintendent and had him open her apartment so that we could check and see if she was there or not. We had to make sure that she had not collapsed anywhere inside and were somewhat relieved when we found that the apartment was empty. Just as we were leaving the building, one of my mother's neighbors came out to dispose of some garbage, and she told us that my mother had gone to a dance at the senior's community center just up the block.

I was absolutely furious at my mother for being so irresponsible. Not only was I angry with her for causing me personal upset, but I was also angry at her blatant disregard for my guests and for the false alarm that tied up the ambulance and the paramedics. I was angry at the fact that, once again, it had been confirmed to me that I cared for her, even though she didn't care for me. I marched up the block to the community center, where I found her all dressed up with her hair and nails done, ready to spend the night dancing. I looked her straight in the eye and said, "Where do you get off calling my home, saying you can't breathe, then hanging up the phone, and immediately leaving your apartment to come here to dance?" She didn't say a word to me. She just looked at me, and seeing that I wasn't going to get a response from her, I asked her, "What did you think that I would do?" At that very moment, my mind was flooded with many memories of my childhood, of the many times that I had come to her rescue. The fact that I had so often come to her rescue was such an enigma when you consider that all through my childhood, she had never once come to my rescue when I was in a time of need. Because I had carried these feelings with me into my adult life, I had developed my own doctrine in this area which went like this. "She didn't, so I will."

A perfect example of how this worked was the manner in which I had handled buying clothing for my son. When I was young, my mother didn't provide me with adequate clothing, so when I had my son, I bought him 5 of everything. There was absolutely no balance. I carried this method of operations around with me for years, not realizing what it really was, nothing more than a curse that we live what we learn. Yet regardless of how I felt or how I hurt, she was still my mom, and she was still complaining about having difficulty breathing. So, I called for an ambulance once again, and when it arrived, it was the same one that had gone to her apartment building earlier. When the two paramedics learned that my mother was the woman they couldn't find earlier, they made sure that she knew how displeased they were at not being able to find her. They made sure that she got the message loud and clear that while they were answering a false alarm, they might have been delayed in answering a real emergency.

After completing their preliminary medical examination of my mother, the paramedics took her to the emergency department of Oshawa General Hospital. Upon our arrival, the emergency doctor examined her right away in order to establish why my mother was having difficulty breathing. After receiving the results of her initial blood tests, the doctor told us that my mother was not in any immediate danger but that he wanted to do more tests. In order for the doctor to properly diagnose what exactly had happened, he would have to take six additional blood samples from my mother, each sample one hour apart. Since this special test would require my mother to stay at the hospital for seven hours, and since we still had a house full of guests, I told the nurse that we would leave my mother in her care. I asked her to call me at home when the test was completed, and I would come back to the hospital, pick up my mother and drive her home. At about 11:00 pm that evening the nurse called to inform me that my mother had signed herself out of the hospital and that she had taken a cab home. She stated that the doctor had been unable to make his diagnosis due to the fact that the blood test was incomplete. As soon as I got off the phone, I called my mother at home to ask her why she had not stayed at the hospital to complete the test. She responded to me by saying, "I didn't have time to hang around there because I had to do my hair." I guess I should have known better than to ask. After all, what else would she have to do at 11:00 pm in the evening but her hair? During our telephone conversation, the only positive thing she said to me was that she was feeling a lot better. I couldn't help thinking that she was such a stubborn woman and that she just did not want to sit still for anything or anyone.

With the root cause of her sickness not properly identified, her condition did not improve. It only got worse. With my mother's inability to swallow now affecting her ability to eat, she was now limited to drinking a liquid food supplement called "Ensure." Over the next few weeks, my mother had numerous appointments with both doctors and specialists, yet there was no visible improvement in her condition. She began to show signs of excessive weight loss as well as being very weak and having no energy. In addition to these symptoms, she was having great difficulty walking any distance at all. Her solution to this situation was to buy herself an electric scooter. After all, she had places to go and things to do, and she was quite determined that nothing was going to slow her down.

As time passed, her speech continued to deteriorate, and due to a lack of proper nutrition, her memory was also starting to fail. Even though she was becoming weaker by the day, my mother continued to go out riding on her scooter. It was evident by the number of bruises, cuts, and scrapes that she had on her body that she had tipped the scooter and fallen off it a number of times. She would often go out on her scooter, become disoriented, and eventually end up lost. On more than one occasion, a total stranger would find her and call the building where she lived to have one of her friends come and pick her up. Her scooter riding days were cut short when she was found riding her scooter along a major highway, heading away from Oshawa towards the town of Bowmanville. She was found stopped at the side of the road, disoriented and lost, badly sunburned and suffering from heat exhaustion. The gentleman who found her called the police and tended to her immediate needs until they arrived. Seeing the condition she was in, the police picked up her and her scooter and drove her to Oshawa General Hospital for treatment and evaluation. The moment I received the call from the hospital to tell me that my mother had been admitted, I jumped into my van and drove to Oshawa.

Upon arriving at the hospital, the doctor told me that he had examined my mother and had found that she was extremely malnourished, so a feeding tube would have to be inserted into her lower bowel. When I saw the condition she was in, I was quite appalled and could hardly believe how much weight she had lost in such a short period of time. My mother's weight usually hovered around the 130-pound mark, yet in spite of losing over 30-pound, she was still a going concern. She just wasn't going to quit. After several days in the hospital, my mother was released and allowed to go home to her apartment. The staff at the hospital had made arrangements for a V.O.N. nurse to visit her every day to help her hook up her feeding tube. We also had one of her friends, a retired registered nurse who lived in the same building as her, keep close tabs on her. Almost two weeks passed before we found out that my mother had been missing her daily feedings due to the fact that she was never home when the V.O.N. nurse called to see her. When I confronted my mother about this, she had all the excuses in the world for why she wasn't home, the major one being that she had to go shopping.

Since my mother was in the habit of carrying a large sum of cash in her wallet at all times, it became quite a concern for us, particularly since her condition was getting much worse. Our concerns proved to be valid when one day, after being at the hairdresser, she stopped in to have a quick look through the local Goodwill store. In a moment of forgetfulness, she put her purse down to look at something, forgot to pick it up, and left the store, leaving her purse behind. When she realized what she had done, she went back to the store, only to find that although her wallet was still in her purse, all her money had been stolen out of it. When she told me what had happened, it was quite obvious that she was very upset about it, no doubt due to the fact that this had been a very expensive lesson for her as she had over $650 in her wallet.

Unfortunately, the downhill spiral continued, and my mother's condition got progressively worse. She had gone out on her scooter and got lost again, and once again, the police were called to pick her up and transport her to the hospital. When the doctor at the hospital saw her deteriorated condition, he concluded that she was no longer able to care for herself and should be in a nursing home. My mother's weight had continued to drop, and she now only weighed 89 pounds.

After the doctor consulted with us, he officially declared my mother incompetent. This course of action was followed to enable the doctor to keep her in the hospital until the social worker could convince her that she required constant care.

What happened next was totally unexpected, and it caught everyone by surprise, even the security staff at the hospital. Even though my mother's scooter riding days had come to an end, she had apparently decided that nobody was going to hold her down, so she carried out the first of three escape attempts from the hospital. One afternoon, at the end of the visiting hours, she casually walked to the elevator amid a group of visitors who were leaving. Upon exiting the elevator on the ground floor, she simply walked out the front doors of the hospital. She left the hospital grounds and walked all the way home in her nightgown and slippers. When the hospital staff finally realized she was missing, the police were informed, and they picked her up as she was trying to get in the front door of her apartment building. I understand that she surrendered without a fuss and went quietly as the police officers returned her to the hospital.

Escape attempt number two happened a day later and was almost a duplicate of attempt number one. Once again, the police were called, and once again, they picked her up as she was trying to get in the front door of her apartment building.

Not about to give up, my mother made a third and final attempt which prompted the hospital administration to insist that she have a psychological examination to determine her ability to recognize that she was doing harm to herself. As a result of this examination, she was immediately assigned a personal security guard who was placed outside her hospital room door. My mother really liked her security guard because he was young and cute and because two or three times a day, he would take her out to the park in her wheelchair. In spite of the differences that I had with my mother, it was very difficult for me to watch her losing control of her life like this, even though it was for her own safety.

19

Standing in The Gap

I can honestly say that both the doctors and the staff at Oshawa General Hospital did their very best to get my mother's weight back up to where it should be, but, despite their efforts, her weight continued to drop. By this time, I was becoming increasingly concerned about her as I could see that her body mass was decreasing rapidly and that she was literally fading away to nothing. Unfortunately, my mother had learned how to disconnect her feeding tube from the dispensing machine, and she thought nothing of disconnecting herself and going for a walk around the large common area on the floor. She seemed to be oblivious to the fact that as she did this, she was dripping food from her feeding tube all over the floor while her dispensing machine continued to pump out food all over the floor in her room. While my mother's actions were not rational, I truly believe that she was not oblivious to what she was doing. I also don't believe that she had a death wish and wanted to die and that her actions were a deliberate attempt to accelerate the process. Knowing my mother as I did, I believe that she just felt trapped and that her actions were a response to her desire to be free of the limitations that she was now experiencing.

While I was going through this situation with my mother, I was very fortunate to have the full support of my friend, Beverley. The truth is, if she had not been there for me, I probably would have "crashed and burned" and may not have made it through. She was with me every step of the way and basically walked through this whole process with me, providing me with all the encouragement and support that I required.

One afternoon the Lord dropped it in my spirit that I should ask my mother to forgive me of anything I had ever said or done that might have caused her any hurt or offense. When I told Beverley what I had been led to do, she said, "Yes, Sharon, you should do just that." Because of how my mother had treated me in the past, I really had mixed emotions about the whole thing. I wasn't quite sure how I should do it, so I had no choice but to pray and ask the Lord to show me the way. By this time, my mother could not speak at all, and the only way we could communicate was by using simple sign language or by writing notes to each other. Even this was becoming more and more difficult as her handwriting had become quite illegible and almost impossible to read. When Beverley and I went to the hospital the next day, I sat down beside my mother's bed and wrote her a short letter.

Dear Mom,

Please forgive me for anything that I have ever said to you or done to you in my life that has caused you hurt or pain. I love you Mom, and furthermore, I choose to forgive you for all that has happened between you and me, that has caused me hurt and offense.

When I had finished writing the letter, I immediately passed it over to Beverley so she could proofread it to ensure that the wording was okay and that there was nothing in it that was inappropriate. After she read the letter, she passed it back to me, nodding her head to let me know that it was okay to give it to my mother. I then handed the letter to my mother, and as I watched her read it, I saw her eyes fill up with tears. When she had finished reading, she looked up at me with that sheepish look that she had and nodded her head to let me know that she had forgiven me. She then motioned to me that she needed a piece of paper and a pen, which I handed over to her. She began to write, and when she had finished, she passed me the paper. She had written the five words that I had been longing to hear or read for years. When I read, "Sharon, will you forgive me?" I looked up at her and said, "Yes, Mom, I forgive you." Since she could no longer speak, she then crossed her arms over her chest as this was the only way she could tell me that she loved me. I said to her, "Yes, Mom, I know that you love me, and I love you."

That day I spent with my mother in Oshawa General Hospital was one of the toughest days I had ever lived through, yet even though it was tough, it was a good day. The words and feelings that were exchanged between my mother and me that day helped break off the chains of bondage that had held me back for so long. Glory to God! A week or so later, my mom was transferred from Oshawa General Hospital into a long-term care facility located in Whitby, not far from our home. Because of her reputation as an escape artist at the Oshawa General Hospital, the administrator decided to place her in the secure wing of the facility in order to minimize her opportunity to wander. The staff members were really very good with her, and they made sure that she was taken out into the garden at least a couple of times every day. Unfortunately, my mom wasn't too happy with being locked up all the time, and even though I knew it was for her own good, I must admit that I felt bad for her. Every other day, when Beverley and I would go to visit with her, we would also take her outside in her wheelchair if the weather was warm enough. Throughout this whole process, what I really found amazing was the change in my attitude toward my mom.

When I was young, my mother would make me put her hair up in rollers and paint her nails, and I came to hate doing that for her. I guess I felt that way because I knew that when her hair and nails were done, it usually meant that she was going out and that I would be left home alone as usual. Now, as part of my healing process, God had seemingly given me the ability to love and care for her as never before in this, her time of need. At her request, I would wash her hair and put it up in rollers, paint her nails and take her out for walks. I was actually more than happy to do these things for her. My mother always liked to look her best, and it brought her great comfort when, once a week, I would make an appointment for her to have her hair done by a hairdresser that came right into the hospital ward. She really enjoyed having her hair done, and knowing that she looked good definitely raised her spirits and made her feel better. I continued to take home her dirty laundry so that I could wash it for her, to make it nice and soft, as I didn't want industrial laundry soap residue rubbing against her skin. As the days became weeks, she became even frailer as she was still removing her feeding tube, causing her weight to drop to 67 pounds.

I had made my mother a promise that one day when the weather was better, I would take her down to the lake in her wheelchair. Well, that day finally came, a day when it wasn't raining and it wasn't too cold, and the promise that I had made had to be kept. So it was that Beverley and I wheeled Mom in her wheelchair down to the shores of Lake Ontario, and as we were walking, Beverley spoke quietly to me, saying, "Sharon, it's important for you to fulfill this promise to her, isn't it?" I replied, "Yes, it is Beverley. Mom made so many promises to me when I was little, and so many were never kept." I knew this was something that I needed to do, not just for her but also for me.

It was a very quiet, uneventful walk down to the lake, but on the way back, my mom noticed some bulrushes at the edge of the water. She motioned to us that she wanted one to take one back with her, so I crossed the road and gingerly stepped towards the bulrushes, trying not to get my feet too wet as I stepped on the marshy soil. There I was, sinking in the mud while trying to pull out a single bulrush whose roots had obviously gone all the way through to China. When it finally came free, I almost fell on my backside, and as I recovered my balance and looked up, there across the road were Beverley and my mom, both laughing their heads off at my efforts. Beverley shouted over to me that my mom wanted a second bulrush. I said to her, "You want me to go back in there for another one? You must be kidding." All I could do was laugh with them as I went back in and retrieved a second bulrush, thinking to myself that all they really wanted was to see me falling in the mud. As the weather began to change and the temperature dropped, we quickly made our way back to the hospital with Mom and her two bulrushes, both of which were much bigger than she was. As we went made our way through the secure doors of her ward, the nurses all smiled and laughed. "That's your Mom," they said.

Knowing that her time was getting short and realizing that Julia hadn't seen her nannie for some time, I decided to bring her with me on my next visit to the hospital. When we walked through the doors, and my mom saw Julia, she immediately went to the snack cart with the puddings on it and motioned to the nurse that she wanted one for her granddaughter. This would be the last time that Julia would see her nannie, and I was so glad for both of them that it was a good visit, in spite of the difficulty my mom was having trying to communicate with us.

It was late in the evening, about one week later, when I received a call from the nurse's station at the hospital to inform me that my mother had taken a bit of a fall. The nurse I was speaking to on the phone informed me that she had hurt her hip and that the doctor had been called in to check her out. Nothing was broken, and she was resting just fine. When I got off the phone, I looked at my husband and said to him, "I don't think she will last too much longer." He agreed with me, and with that, I went downstairs to the kitchen to get myself a drink before going to bed. During the last few weeks of her life, I had come to realize that my mother had indeed accepted Jesus as her Lord and personal Saviour. While knowing this gave me some peace, I did have a moment of insecurity as I was standing in the kitchen. As a wave of uncertainty passed over me, I just felt Holy Spirit leading me to me pray.

"Father, in the name of Jesus, I stand in the gap and repent on behalf of my mother for anything that would stand between you and her. Please forgive her Father. Amen."

After I had finished my drink, I went back upstairs to my husband's office and told him what had just happened in the kitchen. He didn't say too much at the time, just that he believed that I had done the right thing by following the leading of the Holy Spirit. It was almost 11:00 pm and time for bed. We weren't in bed for more than two minutes when the phone rang. Expecting the worst, I picked up the phone to find the doctor from the hospital on the other end of the line. She began with, "I'm sorry, Sharon, but your Mom has passed on." As she explained to me that my mother had not been in any pain and that she had just gone to sleep and had passed away quietly, my emotions began to go wild. On the one hand, I wasn't surprised to receive the call, and in some ways, I was quite relieved that it was all over for her. But on the other hand,

I cried because she was gone, especially since I had just started to have a good relationship with her. When I finally settled down, I began to realize that I was so blessed that my Father in Heaven had allowed me to spend the best six weeks that I ever had with my mom.

I can't deny that I did feel some guilt and remorse at not having gone to visit my mom that afternoon. All sorts of thoughts ran through my head about what I could have done and what I should have done. I also regretted the fact that I hadn't gone to the hospital that evening after receiving the call about her fall. Having been assured by the nurse that she was resting comfortably, I figured that I would see her the next afternoon. But now that she was gone, I felt that I should have been there with her, that she should not have died alone. When I told my husband what was going through my mind, he was very comforting to me, assuring me that I need not feel guilty because she wasn't alone at the time of her passing. He said this to me, "Sharon, God was right there with her at the very moment of her passing because in His word it is written, 'I will never leave you nor forsake you.'"

Hebrews 13:5

5: Keep your lives free from the love of money and be content with what you have, because God has said, "Never will I leave you; never will I forsake you."

So, it is written in His word that on the 10th of October 2001, my mom wasn't alone when she went to be with Jesus. When I got up the next morning, the first thing I did was call the secretary at the church to let her know that my mom had passed on the night before. I also asked her to tell Pastor Dan and Pastor Ruth when they came in and to update anyone who called to enquire how my mother was doing. Bob and I went directly to the funeral home to make all the necessary arrangements, and while we were waiting for all the paperwork to be processed, in walked our friend, Pastor Dan.

When Pastor Dan had arrived at the church and heard the news of my mom's passing, he immediately came down to the funeral home to support us. He was a little upset at us because we had not called him when we had received the news the night before. When I told him that we hadn't wanted to bother anyone that late at night, he looked at me and said, "Don't be silly, Sharon. We are here for you." It was a real blessing for us to have such support from someone who loved us. Two days later, we held a small memorial service for my mother at our church, which was attended by family and a few of her close friends. The ministry staff at Christian Life Centre stepped up to the plate, with Pastor Dan taking the service and the others offering their support by catering a small luncheon for those in attendance. After the service, as Pastor Ruth took me in her arms to give me a hug, I shared with her what had happened in the kitchen that night. She looked at me and said, "You, my little honey, stood and bridged the gap between your mother and God. What an awesome privilege."

As I concluded writing this chapter, Holy Spirit reminded me of that scripture in 1st Corinthians.

1 Corinthians 15:55

55: "Where, O death, is your victory? Where, O death, is your sting?"

20

My Daughter

I now began a new chapter in my life where I found myself spending more and more time alone with the Lord. He began to speak to me in great depth, showing me the many areas in my life that still required some healing. One of these areas was regarding my daughter, Julia, whose behavior was causing me some concern. In the past, I had always wondered why Julia was so sensitive, why she spent so much time on her own, and why she did not seem to get along well with others. I had expected her to grow out of these practices, but even though she was getting older, she continued to behave as she always had. The Lord began to show me that Julia had learned all she was doing, how she was behaving, and how she was responding to others by watching me. She had seen my fears, my lack of faith, and my way of handling situations, and my ways had become her ways. The adage, "Children don't always do what you tell them. They do what they see you do!" jumped out at me, and I saw for the first time in my life how my practices had affected my daughter.

The Lord began to show me the common thread that ran through all the questions I had been asking Him. He began by showing me the circumstances and events that had brought about my teaching my daughter how to walk in the fear that I had walked in. God showed me in what could only be described as a vision; it was an instant replay of an incident that had taken place a few years before when I used to have a daycare in my home. One evening, when Buzz, Julia's dad, arrived home from work, Julia had run to the door to meet him. As she ran to the door, in one smooth action, my daycare employee caught her by the arm, swung her around, and slapped her across the face. This action was justified by my employee as punishment for running in the house, a measure of punishment that was never used on any of the other children. The way I had handled that situation was completely wrong as I chose not to deal with the offender, my employee, but to begin a process of continually protecting Julia.

My initial reaction to the daycare incident was to protect Julia by creating a series of detours that would keep her out of the daycare altogether. I would tell her to go upstairs and put on a movie, to draw some pictures or read a book, to do something, anything at all that would prevent her from coming into the daycare. Rather than confront the issue and deal with my employee, my way of protecting Julia was to exclude her from being anywhere near the daycare. The Lord basically showed me that because I had not dealt with my fear, I had created a situation that caused me to isolate my daughter. My actions had excluded her from having any interaction with the other children in the daycare. The fact that Julia had begun reading at age three was a positive thing, but now that she was burying herself in her books. They were becoming her life, and this was causing me some serious concerns. I felt bad because I had been so afraid of having any kind of confrontation with my employee. And I felt responsible for driving Julia out of the real world into her own little world.

The Lord then showed me that she had never been allowed or taught how to play with others because, when she did come out of her room to play, I was always attached to her hip to make sure nobody hurt her. I was Julia's protector, and if Julia and another child ever had a dispute, she would usually overreact, and I would immediately quiet her down and tell her not to say anything. I would tell her to do what I would do, let it go, just as I had remained quiet and let it go when my employee stepped over her boundaries. It was bad enough that I walked on eggshells in my own home, but what was worse was the fact that I allowed my employee to influence how I handled my daughter. I was so busy trying to avoid a situation where my employee would step in and say or do something that I lost sight of the fact that Julia was being affected in such a negative way. When the lights finally came on, when I fully realized that Julia had seen how I had handled all these situations and how as a result, it had begun a process in her that would cause her to grow up just like me, I cried out, "God help me!"

As painful as it was for me to deal with, to make things right, I continued to seek the Lord for both the answers and direction I needed. I accepted the fact that I was responsible for Julia being the way she was, having trained her for years to have and walk in a victim mentality. The Lord began to show me the patterns of behavior that Julia was prone to, her M.O. for handling different situations. For example, when Julia would come home from school and complain about a problem she was having with a classmate, I would immediately step up to the plate and initiate some action by writing a letter to the teacher, the school principal, or even the school superintendent. Depending upon the situation, sometimes I would make a phone call threatening legal action or police involvement. In general, I made a whole lot of fuss that sometimes worked and sometimes didn't. It's strange how I had no difficulty at all in dealing with the school but all kinds of difficulty dealing with one employee.

As my understanding grew, I began to see the error of my ways as I had never seen it before. It was difficult for me, and I was far from happy, especially since it was now so apparent to me that my way of handling Julia's issues had been drastically wrong. It was bad enough that I wasn't handling the school issues correctly, but what made it worse was that I was handling other issues the same way. For example, when Julia would go over to a friend's house to play, and a situation arose while she was there, I would immediately place the blame on that family rather than look at Julia or myself. The truth is that Julia couldn't handle any kind of confrontation at all because she had never been taught how and had never been allowed the experience of dealing with confrontation. Every time someone gave her a hard time or picked on her, she would just come running to Mommy with the expectation that I would take care of it. This was what the Lord was trying to show me, that this cycle had to be broken if Julia was to walk in freedom, and God knows she has been called to walk in that freedom.

You have no doubt heard that old expression, "God will take you around the same mountain again and again until you get it right." I must admit that I knew that mountain very well and had absolutely no desire to go around it again. The Lord brought me to the place where I realized that when you teach a child how to become a victim, you literally bring death to their self-esteem and any sense of self-worth they might have. When self-esteem and self-worth die, self-pity and the "poor me" syndrome begin to grow. This opens the door to many lies of the enemy, such as "Nobody loves you," "You're all alone," and "Nobody cares."

As for me, I never thought for a moment that the way I was raising my daughter would expose her to all this garbage and cause her to be influenced by such strongholds. Even though at this time I had been saved for over six years, it was obvious to me that I was still walking in many of my old ways, and my daughter was walking right alongside me. What the Lord really impressed upon me was this; that we who profess to be Christians should not be walking in a victim mentality. Why? Because His word says that we are victors and that we walk in the power and authority that He has given us. We are victorious through Christ, who died for us on the cross at Calvary, because in His death, there is victory, and in His resurrection, there is power. We are victorious as He is victorious because He lives in us through the presence of the Holy Spirit, the same Holy Spirit that raised Him from the dead. Hallelujah!

Now that my eyes were opened to this, I was distraught by the fact that I had allowed this situation to evolve and perpetuate the way it had over the years. I cried, and I cried, and I cried; it was horrible. I had such pain and hurt inside of me, and through my tears, I could also feel all my daughter's pain. I said to the Lord, "God forgive me, and please show me how to teach her to be victorious and not to become a victim." As I prayed, I also asked the Lord to supernaturally begin to deliver Julia from her pain, and that is exactly what He did.

As God continued to work over the next two years, we walked in an abundance of mercy and grace as He placed us in situation after situation, enabling us to retrain Julia in many areas of her life. It seemed that every time Julia would visit a friend to play, a dispute would start. My fleshly reaction was to jump to the rescue, primarily because in my childhood, nobody had ever come to my rescue. It was very hard for me as a mom to learn to step back and allow my child to deal with conflict herself. But I realized that I was allowing her to gain experience and to grow from the situation.

A couple of weeks later, I was having a heart-to-heart conversation with Linda, a lady who was both a close friend and one of my spiritual mentors. As I poured out my heart and shared my newfound revelation with her, she smiled and told me that for some time, she had been praying for both Julia and me. It turned out that Linda had been praying specifically for me for over a year, praying that God would bring me the revelation that I needed and that He would open my eyes to the truth. She began to share with me many of her personal feelings towards Julia. She told me that there was a time when she was afraid to have Julia over to her house to play because she knew that if a situation or a dispute occurred between Julia and one of her children that I would always blame her children. She knew I would always take the stance that it was never my daughter who was in the wrong, that I would get angry with her and her kids and even angrier with Julia for causing me to be angry with them. Now that Linda had made me aware of her feelings, over the next few months, as I became stronger in the Lord and able to receive it, she would drop the occasional timely word of direction and encouragement.

Having stepped back and allowed Julia to become her own person, I have had a number of people come up to me a say, "What a change I have seen in Julia. Has she ever grown?" Yes, Julia has grown. She has grown in so many areas, and many of the issues that once troubled her are no more. They are gone because she is not the person she once was, and neither am I. As I have walked through this process, I have learned that God is truly "No respecter of persons" and that He will use anything, anyone, and any situation to help bring about His plans and purposes for someone's life.

Throughout this difficult process, God has taught me how to address the root cause of a situation rather than get angry and upset at the individuals involved in it. Instead of getting upset at the situation and with Julia, I now sit down with her and ask her what the word of God says about her. Then I asked her what Jesus would do if He found himself in the same situation that she now finds herself in. By following this process, I have been able to begin to teach Julia how to evaluate a situation and to reason out what would be the appropriate course of action for her to take and with whom to take it. Thankfully she has acquired the ability to see the big picture, and now, at eleven years of age, she is more than capable of thinking for herself. The Lord has allowed a few situations to take place in Julia's life as part of His plan to set her free, and even though this process is a God thing, the process of walking free has not been easy for her. It hasn't been easy for me either, although I can now honestly say that I know God is with her, holding her hand and walking her into freedom, for His word says, "He will never leave us nor forsake us," Glory to God!

Now that I have released Julia into the hands of God, she is becoming the young woman of God that He has called her to be. As her mother, I will continue to pray for her supernatural deliverance, secure in the knowledge that it will surely happen. After all, is said and done, the word of God says, "Ask, and you shall receive." So, in accordance with His word, I have continued to ask God to show me any other areas in my life that need to be dealt with, and, as always, He has been faithful to do so!

21

Awakening

As I began to write this chapter, I found myself asking God, "When will you ever be finished with me?" It was one of those silly questions that really did not require an answer because I already knew that the answer was "Never!" Being the person that I am, having such a desire and passion for the things of God, I continually ask God to enable me to grow and mature into the woman of God that He has called me to be. I have learned through firsthand experience that God is more than able to fulfill my desires and answer my prayers, particularly when they are in line with what He wants for my life.

My awakening began during one of our Friday night ministry sessions, where I had felt led to ask a couple of the members of the group to pray for me. Two beautiful women of God, Linda, and Joanne, came and placed their hands on me and began to pray. As they prayed and sought God for his Word and direction for me, I waited silently, wondering what God would have to say to me tonight. What happened next came as a real shock to my system when Joanne stopped praying and spoke to me, saying, "Sharon, you're walking in rebellion." "Excuse me," I said. "You must be kidding". Linda then spoke up and said, "Joanne is right, Sharon. You are." "What do you mean I'm walking in rebellion?" I asked, "Who, me? No way! Remember, I am the woman who teaches others not to walk in rebellion," I stated emphatically. However, I was about to discover that I was just like so many that I had ministered to, that I was just as blind to the error of my own ways as they were to theirs. I was also about to discover that it was God's timing for me to recognize them and deal with them.

There I was, standing out there in full view of everyone, totally exposed and feeling quite uncomfortable. After all, in my position of leadership in the Friday night group, I was accustomed to having a measure of control over what took place. I looked at them both and said, "Okay! If God says so, in what way am I walking in rebellion?" They both answered at the same time, saying, "To God and to your husband." "What do you mean"? I exclaimed, not being able to grasp the fact that I was so blind to this that I couldn't see what was happening. I remember thinking to myself, "God, I love you so much. How can this be so?" As far as my husband was concerned, we had had our ups and downs, just like any married couple. There were times when I felt that he was not taking care of me the way he should, and I had been very upfront in telling him what I thought of his performance in that area. Then I said to Linda and Joanne, "Okay, ladies. Let's go. Get on with it. If this is God's plan, hurry up and get on with it."

Then with such gentleness, they both repeated to me what they had previously said, that I needed to walk in submission to God and to my husband. My response to them was clear and concise, "Okay. God, Yes! Husband, No!" Linda then said to me, "God's plan, Sharon, is for you to walk in submission to Him and to your husband". By this time, I was more than a little upset, and I responded to them with a considerable attitude. "How can you expect me to walk in submission to my husband when in my eyes, he is incapable of protecting and caring for me?" I began to cry because I was afraid of being hurt again, yet I wanted to be obedient to God. But how was I going to do that? Linda spoke up, saying, "I know and understand how you feel, Sharon, because I have been through this already." She shared with me from her own experience how, when she had been in the same position that I now found myself in, she had argued with God for weeks. The result of all of her arguing with God was given; she did not get her own way. God got His own way because He is God. Linda continued to say, "Sharon, God will walk with you all the way. He will show you how just as he has done in every other area of your life."

I was absolutely terrified of doing what they said I should do, even though I knew that it was the right thing, that it was a must for me! As Linda and Joanne continued in prayer for me, they prayed that God would give me all the strength, wisdom, and understanding that it would take for me to get through this. As they were praying for me, I glanced up to see my husband walking behind the three of us. I immediately thought to myself that he must have been listening to what was being said. Believing that he must be enjoying my total discomfort, I turned and said to him, "Stop gloating." He never said a word in response and just kept walking. As I went to sit down, Linda followed me and said, "Sharon, he wasn't gloating. He was praying in the Spirit for you." "Yeah, right," I thought. "After all that has happened, how am I supposed to trust my husband to protect me and to look after me?" Suddenly, the lights came on, and I immediately realized that I was looking at myself for all the answers, not at God. The situation I was dealing with was beyond my ability to resolve, and it was going to take God Himself to sort this one out. All that I would be required to do was to get myself out of His way.

With the ministry over for the evening, as Bob and I drove home from the church, my mind was racing with everything that had happened that night. When we arrived home, I immediately excused myself, went to the office, shut the door, fell to my knees, and repented of my actions. Not fully understanding everything that was happening, I cried out to God, "I need you to show me Lord." Well, He answered my prayer by bringing back to my memory something that I had asked and prayed for a number of times in the past. It was a verse of scripture from Psalm 139.

Psalm 139:24

24: "See if there is any offensive way in me, and lead me in the way everlasting."

On many occasions, my husband Bob has told me that I pray dangerously, and it appeared that I was once again guilty of doing so. As always, God came through and answered my prayers, even though they were not the answers I was looking for. He told me, first, that it was not my job to try and change my husband. I was to give him over to God so that He could change him. What had happened was that my pride had gotten in the way, and I had fallen into the trap of believing that I could do a better job of changing my husband than God could. I also came to the realization that all through my marriage to Bob, I had concentrated on all the bad and not seen enough of the good. I had placed expectations on my husband, and because he was a pastor, I had convinced myself that sooner or later, he would get it right, with me helping God out in that process, of course.

Somewhere along the way, I had lost sight of the fact that my husband was only human and that although he was a pastor, he was not perfect. After all, only God is perfect. I also came to the realization that we ladies all too often place expectations on our husbands that they are completely unaware of. All too often, we have said to them, "This is how it should have been done! You should have known better! I shouldn't have to tell you!" And then, after having expounded such great knowledge and wisdom to them, our usual reward is a blank stare and a "Yes, Dear," which should come as no surprise because men don't think the way that women do. I love the comment that my friend Linda once made to me. She said, "Men are like waffles. They keep everything in separate boxes, while we women are like spaghetti. We get everything all tangled up." Some time ago, I received an e-mail that included a letter from God to women, and I think it fits in here perfectly.

A Letter from God to Women - Author Unknown

When I created the heavens and the earth, I spoke them into being. When I created man, I formed him and breathed life into his nostrils.

But you, woman, I fashioned after I breathed the breath of life into man because your nostrils are too delicate. I allowed a deep sleep to come over him so I could patiently and perfectly fashion you. Man was put to sleep so he could not interfere with the creativity.

From one bone, I fashioned you. I chose the bone that protects man's life. I chose the rib, which protects his heart and lungs and supports him as you are meant to do. Around this one bone, I shaped you..... I modeled you. I created you perfectly and beautifully. Your characteristics are as the rib, strong yet delicate and fragile. You provide protection for the most delicate organ in man, his heart. His heart is the center of his being; his lungs hold the breath of life. The rib cage will allow itself to be broken before it will allow damage to the heart. Support man as the rib cage supports the body. You were not taken from his feet to be under him, nor were you taken from his head to be above him. You were taken from his side to stand beside him and be held close to his side.

You are my perfect angel...

You are my beautiful little girl.

You have grown to be a splendid woman of excellence,

and my eyes fill when I see the virtues in your heart.

Your eyes…don't change them.

Your lips, how lovely they are when they part in prayer.

Your nose is so perfect in form.

Your hands…so gentle to touch.

I've caressed your face in your deepest sleep.

I've held your heart close to mine.

Of all that breathes, you are most like me. Adam walked with me in the cool of the day, yet he was lonely. He could not see me or touch me. He could only feel me. So everything I wanted Adam to share and experience with me I fashioned in you: my holiness, my strength, my purity, my love, my protection, and support. You are special because you are an extension of me.

Man represents my image, Woman my emotions. Together you represent the totality of God. So man treat woman well, Love her and respect her, for she is fragile.

Even though I was still in much fear of being hurt yet again, God began His process of walking me out of the self-inflicted bondage I had allowed myself to be caught up in. My life experiences had taught me that no one had ever protected me or come to my defense, and because of this belief based on experience, I had become quite proficient at taking care of myself. One of the tactics I had developed to protect myself from hurt and pain was to point out every area of my husband's life where I felt he was in error. Every time the opportunity presented itself, I made sure that I corrected him. When we argued, I told him that he was self-centered, arrogant, and full of pride. Then after telling him like it was, I would walk away, thinking, even believing, that he had it all wrong and I had it all right.

Meanwhile, God, in His infinite wisdom, had continued to allow situations to arise while I, not realizing what I was doing, continued on my path of destruction. Blinded to see what was going on, I continued to run my husband down, having nothing good to say about him, his walk with God, or his relationship with me, or anyone else for that matter. On many occasions, I criticized him for making what I considered to be negative comments. I told him that if anything positive ever came out of his mouth, I might die of shock. During one dispute we had, I even told him that if he didn't straighten up his act, it would cost him everything, his family, his job, and worse yet, his ministry. When I look back at those situations, I find myself wondering how I ever expected my husband to grow with God when I, his wife, was cutting him down with every word that came out of my mouth. When I look back and see to what extent God allowed me to go to before coming to my rescue, it scares me. But come to my rescue, He did. Glory to God.

One Thursday morning, I was sitting in my family room, where I was watching Joyce Meyers on the television. As she taught that morning, I saw all the bits and pieces fall into place, and I received the direction I was looking for. It was amazing how the Holy Spirit confirmed what I already knew in my heart, enabling me to see what God wanted me to do. The process had actually begun some months before when God had laid it upon my heart to do foster care in our home. Now that everything was confirmed, we set up two bedrooms, each with two single beds, to enable us to take a family of four. After a period of doing relief for other full-time families, we finally got the call asking us to take on a family of three, a nine-year-old boy, a four-year-old girl, and a seven-week-old baby boy. I was so excited when we got the word that we were going to have our own foster children. When they arrived, accompanied by their social worker, it was obvious that they had been badly neglected and abused. Because of my own childhood, my heart was deeply touched by their condition. As I took care of these children, feeding them, keeping them clean, and loving them, I began to see them as my own.

After a few weeks, their mother was allowed access to them, something I really wasn't too happy about, considering the fact that they had been taken away from her because she had not cared for them properly. When they had arrived at our home, they were hungry, dirty, and had absolutely no personal belongings with them at all. Now I was the one who fed them, bathed them, and bought them new clothes. I had purchased car seats for the two younger ones and a new stroller for our little man. To get them ready for their first supervised visit with their mother, I bathed them and got them dressed up in their new clothes, and they all looked cute. As arranged by Children's Services, one of their drivers picked them up at our house and drove them to the Toronto location where their mother was to meet them. After a one-hour supervised visit with their mother and her social worker, the same driver returned the children to my care. When he dropped them off, I noticed right away that the baby boy had been changed out of the outfit that I had sent him in. I really wasn't very happy about that, and I asked the oldest child, a boy, "Why did your mommy change the baby?" He said that his mommy just wanted to see how he looked. The first thing that ran through my mind was that this woman had a lot of nerve when you consider the condition these children were in when they arrived at our home. I was quite offended that she would check out the physical condition of her baby to ensure that he wasn't being mistreated in any way.

I quickly got over my upset and was quite settled until about an hour later when I received a phone call from Bridgeway Family Foster Homes. It was our house worker on the line, and she started the conversation by asking questions about the children. I immediately asked her, "Why all the questions?" "Well, it's like this," she said, "I have just received a report that states that the mother's social worker has great concern about the care the children are receiving. Apparently, when the children had arrived for their visit with their mother, she had immediately undressed the baby to check him out. She found that the baby's ears were dirty, he had a scab under his arm, and, to top it all off, he had a blister on the end of his penis. All these issues have been corroborated by the mother's social worker." Well, I was, as they say, "fit to be tied." I could not believe that this woman, who had lost her children because she had neglected and abused them, had the audacity to make such accusations against me, let alone have them believed and corroborated by her social worker.

To make matters worse, I was instructed by our house worker to take the baby to a doctor for a full physical for the purposes of verifying or disproving the allegations. My immediate response was to tell my house worker that as soon as I made the appointment, I would call her back so she could meet me at the doctor's office. I was quite adamant about having her in attendance as I wanted her to see firsthand that all the allegations were untrue. Of course, the first thing I did when I got off the phone with her was to strip the baby and check him for all the things his mother said were wrong. Not that I was expecting to find anything, but I must admit that I was quite relieved that I did not find anything wrong with him at all. As I was looking under the baby's arm, his older brother came over to the kitchen counter to see what I was doing. He said to me, "This is the arm where my mom found the scab." As I examined the baby's arm, I found no trace of any injury that would have scabbed over. The only thing I found was a piece of black towel fluff from the towel I had used to dry him after his bath that morning. I inspected his ears, where I found no dirt, and I certainly didn't find any blister on the top of his penis.

I must believe that it was a God thing that I was able to get in to see a doctor later that afternoon. By the time I arrived at the doctor's office for my appointment, I was quite a mess. In the presence of our house worker, the doctor performed a full physical on the baby and declared that none of the accusations were true. He wrote on the report form that the baby was perfectly healthy and that he had no concerns at all with respect to the care he was receiving. Having been exonerated of all the allegations made against me, I felt free to let out all the anger that had been welling up within me. I said to our house worker, "Who does this woman think she is, making these accusations against me?" She tried to console me by explaining that this type of situation happened quite often, as the birth mother often views the foster mom as a threat.

In order to prevent a repeat performance, on the children's next visit to see their mother, Bob accompanied me when I drove them into Toronto. We both met with the children's mother, and I took the opportunity to tell her that I was not a threat to her and that we were only taking care of her children for a time to allow her to get her life in order. She told me that she was only concerned for her children, but, having now met me, she was very happy that I was her children's foster mom. Strangely enough, over the next few months that we had her children in our care, we formed a good relationship with her.

When the day finally came that the children were to be reunited with their mother, it was a very sad day for my family. It was difficult because we had accepted these little children into our home, treated them as our own, and they had become part of our family. All during their stay with us, we had walked, talked, and taught them about the love of God and how Jesus had died for their sins. Since they had spent the Christmas season with us, they had so much stuff to take home with them that I volunteered to drive them to their mother's new apartment in the west end of Toronto. While driving them home, Holy Spirit said to me, "Ask them who loves them." When I didn't respond, I heard Holy Spirit say again, "Ask them who loves them." Finally, after being prompted a third time, I said to the children, "Hey guys, who loves you the most?" The boy answered, "Julia." I replied to him, saying, "Yes, Julia loves you, but who loves you the most?" he said, "Jesus loves us the most."

I felt a sense of peace at that moment, I was obedient to God, and any concerns I had about the children going back to their mother were gone. When we finally arrived at their mother's apartment, the family worker was there to meet me and to help unload the children and their belongings. We got everyone and everything loaded into the elevator for the trip up to the third floor and delivered the children to their mother. She was so happy to have them back home with her, and with her family worker present, we said our goodbyes. I hugged the two little ones and told them that I loved them. As I hugged the nine-year-old boy, I told him to be good and to remember that I loved him. As I released my hold on him, he stepped back and made a statement, one I will never forget as long as I live. He said, "I'll never forget that you love us, Sharon, but Jesus loves us the most." I couldn't have been more blessed by seeing his family and the family worker standing in awe of what he had just spoken. I had been used by God to plant the seed in that little boy's heart, and as I left that apartment that day, I prayed, asking God to send another worker to water it and cause it to grow. With all the emotion I was feeling, I had to sit in my van and cry for a while before I was able to drive home.

Let's go back to that Thursday morning, the one I previously mentioned when I was watching Joyce Meyers on television. While she was teaching, she said something to this effect. "Have you ever looked at someone who has just ticked you off and said, who do you think that you're talking to?" I said to myself, "Yes, I've done that." As she continued, Joyce Meyers said that if you have ever reacted in this manner, you were walking in pride. When I heard her say this, the lights finally came on and, although I didn't want to believe what I was hearing, I recognized that it was true. I was walking in pride, and I hadn't recognized it until I heard what Joyce Meyers was teaching. It was now apparent to me that God had been at work, that He had used my experience with the foster children to show me that I was a proud person. I was the one who was walking in pride, the very thing I had accused my husband of doing. Talk about being blind to my own sin. I repented and asked God to forgive me and to help me walk free of this bondage. When my husband arrived home that night, I looked at him and said, "Please forgive me for accusing you of walking in pride". He was quite taken aback at my request and asked me what had happened to cause me to ask his forgiveness. When I told him the whole story of how I had received the revelation, he just smiled, forgave me, and said thank you. As for me, well, I still have a long way to go yet, because pride is a stronghold for many other things, such as arrogance and self-centeredness. You may also recollect that I have previously mentioned the Law of Reciprocity. Well, everything that I had said to my husband came back to me and hit me right between the eyes. The scripture says in Matthew.

Matthew 7:3

3: "Why do you look at the speck of sawdust in your brother's eye and pay no attention to the plank in your own eye?"

As God continues the process of helping me walk out of bondage, He continues to bring to my attention the things in my life that I need to deal with. One evening while my husband Bob and I were out for dinner, God began to show me many hurtful things that I had spoken in error. He brought to my mind the time I had told my husband that if he didn't straighten up his act that it would cost him everything, his family, his job, and, worse yet, his ministry. God showed me that it would not have cost my husband anything, that the cost would have been all mine. When I told Bob what God had shown me, he just laughed and said, "Could you write that down for me, please?"

Since that night, God has made the process much easier for me, and what a process it has been! I have given my husband over to God, and as directed by God, I now pray for him and intercede for him. Having begun to walk in submission to my God and my husband, I have now come under my husband's protective covering where I was supposed to be in the first place. I now experience the security and protection that I have longed for my entire life.

The moment I made the decision to remove myself out of God's way, the moment I stopped trying to help God get it right, was the moment I opened the door to allow Him to answer my prayers. God has been faithful, and I now have a husband who is not only guarding me and protecting me but who is also doing what God has called him to do. Throughout this process, God has so impressed upon me the importance of watching what comes out of our mouths, especially what we say about others. When we recognize sin in other people's lives, instead of talking to others about it, we are to lift them up in prayer and ask God to help them deal with the sin in their lives. We are not to talk about the issues others have; by doing so, we become guilty of spreading rumors and gossip. I now see my husband in a whole new light. I see him as a man of God, a faithful servant of the Most High, a beautiful creation of God. Thank you, Lord!

Please remember this: when we pray to God, asking Him to show us the things in our lives that are not in line with His plan and purpose, He is faithful to do so. If we ask Him to deal with these things, He can only do so if we get out of His way.

22

Friday Nights

As I have already mentioned, at the beginning of October 2001, Bob was asked to teach a four-week course titled Spiritual Gifts as they are outlined in 1st Corinthians chapter 12. It seemed from the very beginning that God only brought in those individuals who truly had a hunger for His Word and were eager to grow spiritually. Due to the lack of understanding on this subject, from the very first night, there were many detours and discussions with many opinions and beliefs to be aired and debated. It was an exciting time for many as the Word of God literally came to life. Many erroneous teachings, perceptions, and beliefs were done away with as the truth shone through. What was even more exciting was that God, through His Holy Spirit, began to move on people's hearts and minds making them open to His Word. There were times when we were in total awe of how He moved, and He did it without any help from either of us. We found out very quickly that if we stepped back and allowed Holy Spirit the freedom to move, so much more was done, and so much more was accomplished. We learned very early on not to push anything, and the result was that many lives were dramatically changed, and many individuals were healed, delivered, and set free. As we allowed Holy Spirit to have total control over the proceedings, we experienced a greater anointing and saw a greater increase in the physical manifestations of the spiritual gifts.

Over the next weeks and months, we would experience many very special evenings. One of my favorites was on week two of the course when on that particular evening, we were quite blessed and delighted when our dear friend, Pastor Ruth, showed up just to see how we were doing and what was going on. She was the one who had initiated my teaching of the motivational gifts and was also responsible for Bob's teaching on the spiritual gifts. A few minutes after she arrived, John, one of our group who was soon to become a regular participant, stood up and said to Bob that the Holy Spirit had told him that we were to lay hands on Pastor Ruth and pray for her. What happened next became a life-changing experience for Pastor Ruth and an invaluable object lesson in obedience for the rest of us who were there. In obedience, we laid hands on her and prayed. We watched in awe as Holy Spirit ministered to her in such a special way by speaking into her spirit the direction and guidance that she had been praying for. In addition, she also received the answers to many personal questions she had been asking the Lord and was absolutely blessed by the whole experience. Pastor Ruth was then released to pray for the other women in the group, and it was a marvelous thing to watch her minister in a new freedom. To see God move in such a way was a great encouragement and faith builder for the members of our small group, and when the four-week course finally ended some twelve weeks later, the group wanted more. With the approval of the church leadership, we continued on with the Friday nights, where we taught a wide range of subjects such as healing, deliverance, anger, offense, faith, the laying on of hands, and the Jezebel spirit, to name a few.

When the Friday nights had been going on for about nine months, a series of circumstances and events that had begun festering some two or three years previously finally came to a head. The result was that the church went through a very difficult time as a small group of people within the church took it upon themselves to come against the Senior Pastor. As the situation unfolded, our Friday night group shifted into intercession mode for the church. It was not unusual for the group to be in the church sanctuary until midnight, praying fervently for the church body and for the leadership. Unfortunately, in just a few short weeks, the situation escalated to the point that it brought about the resignation of our Senior Pastor. When the announcement of his resignation was made to the church, we were also informed that the rest of the Pastoral staff had been asked to resign as well. This caught us totally by surprise, and it was only when we were made aware that it was the policy of the denomination that when the senior

Pastor resigned, there was to be a clean sweep, so allowing the new Pastor to select his own staff. We didn't like it, but we had to accept it. Since Bob and I were in the very unique situation of not being members of the church and not being on the payroll, we were excluded from this clean sweep of the pastoral staff.

During this time, the Friday night group continued in intercession mode, spending much time in prayer for the church and the leadership. Everything happened so quickly that within a period of six weeks, all the pastoral staff was gone, including our primary supporters, Pastor Ruth, and Pastor Dan. This was a very difficult time for us, and due to the upset and distraction that the whole process had created, we actually lost our focus and our way for a short while. It was particularly difficult for me to understand how members of the body of Christ could do what they had done to our Senior Pastor. We had no choice but to give the situation over to God, believing that He would deal will all who were involved, particularly those who had stepped over the line. Despite our difficulties dealing with the loss of our Pastors, God continued to be faithful, and Holy Spirit still showed up to heal, deliver and set us free.

Our friend, Pastor Dan, had been actively involved with an organization called Tahilah and had been assisting in teaching their leadership classes. The classes were held in the evenings on campus at Canada Christian College in Toronto. In the months prior to leaving the church, Pastor Dan had recruited Bob and I to present both the Motivational Gifts and the Spiritual Gifts seminars to the Tahilah leadership classes. Since Pastor Dan knew firsthand the effectiveness of our Friday nights, he now invited us to come and do a "Friday night" or a "Holy Spirit night" for his church leaders-in-training. The whole purpose behind his request was to enable this group of leaders-in-training to see firsthand how the Spirit can move. We immediately recognized this as an opportunity to validate the ministry gifts of our Friday night group, now affectionately known as "The Motley Crew." So, we handpicked a ministry team from the group and, on the arranged date, brought them with us to Canada Christian College.

After an hour of praise and worship, we set them loose on Pastor Dan's leaders-in-training. It was an awesome privilege for us to just stand back and watch while this group of individuals that we had trained and ministered to now minister to others. We were even more delighted to hear the positive response from those ministered to as they confirmed the accuracy of the words spoken over them. The ministry had such an effect on all these leaders-in-training that they recommended to Pastor Dan that the next group have two "Friday nights" during their twelve weeks of training. As for the "Motley Crew", well, they now came to the realization that they were ministers in the truest sense of the word, vessels that God moved on and operated through to further His Kingdom. While in the Spirit, they had imparted and spoken into the lives of these leaders-to-be, bringing direction and revelation to those who were seeking.

It's also interesting to note that our involvement with Tahilah has resulted in some of the participants becoming a part of our Friday night group. As is always the case, word of mouth from those who attend on a regular basis has also brought in others for a night or for a season. When Bob launched his new book, "Healing Revealed," he was invited to promote the book by appearing on "It's A New Day" with Willard Thiessen on Trinity Television Network. Many viewers called in to enquire where they could receive ministry and were directed by Willard's staff on how to contact us. Those who were close enough to our location were invited to come, and some actually came to one of our Friday night ministry sessions, where our "Motley Crew" ministered healing and deliverance to them.

It was always the focus of the Friday night group to seek the face of God and to become equipped to minister under an open heaven. While healing and deliverance are an integral part of God's plan and purpose for the ministry, personal preparation for revival in the church is emerging at a fast pace. Teachings on righteousness, Christ the Redeemer, holy living, repentance, waiting on God, hearing the voice of God, and others are also emerging. We believe that as long as we remain obedient to Holy Spirit, He will continue to move in our midst and manifest the signs and wonders He has promised. As for me, as my Journey continues. I am seeking the face of God daily and am walking in a freedom that is beyond measure. Everything I have can be yours also if you choose to accept it.

23

Here and Now

I began writing this manuscript several years ago, and for a number of reasons, I had to put it aside. In 2003, God stepped in and moved my family from Ontario to British Columbia, where we all went through a period of retraining. This was necessary to prepare us for what He had planned for us. It was like we spent 5-years in a cave, not being recognized for who we were or being allowed to participate in the churches that we attended. By 2008, we had some family issues that caused us to move back to Ontario to involve ourselves in the life of our granddaughter. I was then led to get involved with a Christian foster care organization and found myself caring for three brothers, two of which had special needs. In addition to the three boys, I also had one little girl who was afflicted by Cerebral Palsy. As a family, we were back actively serving in the church, and life was better.

In late 2010 everything changed when one night, I had an encounter with Jesus when He showed up in my bedroom. As I awoke from a deep sleep, I saw Him standing there and heard Him say one word to me, "Mesopotamia." Not fully understanding what that meant, I quickly fell back asleep. Sometime later, Jesus returned again, and again as I awoke from a deep sleep, I heard Him speak that same word, "Mesopotamia." During that night, Jesus showed up five times to speak that one word. When I awoke in the morning, I shared what had happened with my husband, Bob. He immediately went on the computer and Googled Mesopotamia to see if we could get some insight into the meaning. We established that Mesopotamia was the "Crescent-shaped fertile piece of land between the two rivers." Not understanding what Jesus meant with that word, I began to call my church family and my Pastors to ask for their read into what it meant. I must have made a dozen phone calls, and nobody returned my calls. After five days, I eventually came to the realization that God did not want me to get insight from others, He wanted me to ask Him, and that is what I did.

Now that I had understood that God desired me to ask Him the meaning of the word He had delivered, I took my request to prayer. When I did this, I received from Him a number of Scriptures in the book of Isaiah that brought the Revelation of what He was saying.

Isaiah 32:15-20

15: till the Spirit is poured on us from on high, and the desert becomes A fertile field, and the fertile field seems like a forest. 15: The Lord's justice will dwell in the desert, his righteousness live in the fertile field. 17: The fruit of that righteousness will be peace; its effect will be quietness and confidence forever. 18: My people will live in peaceful dwelling places, in secure homes, in undisturbed places of rest. 19: Though hail flattens the forest and the city is leveled completely 20: how blessed you will be, sowing your seed by every stream, and letting your cattle and donkeys range free.

When I asked my husband to read the Scriptures and give me his opinion, all I heard was, **"Oh my God, we're going back."** This was far from what I wanted to hear, as I had said when we left British Columbia that I did not want to return to that God-forsaken place. It is interesting to note that some years before, a close friend gave me a word from the Lord, where I was told that I would be moving to Chilliwack, B.C. It turns out that the farmland in Chilliwack is extremely fertile, is crescent-shaped, and is located between two rivers. Early in December of 2010, we prepared ourselves for our return to British Columbia, planning to be moved to Chilliwack before Christmas. In our journey across Canada, we encountered miracle after miracle, where God moved to protect and make our passage safe. If I ever do a sequel to this book, I will detail the many miracles that we experienced.

Moving forward to 2012, I took a job at the local Mission here in Chilliwack, where I quickly became the "Women's Program Manager. I was extremely comfortable in that position as all my life experiences were being put to good use.

My ability to counsel the women was excellent, primarily because I was able to say to them, "I've been where you're at. I know how you feel because I have felt the hurt and pain that you are feeling." By 2014, my duties were expanded to include "Client Engagement and Assessment." I stayed in that position for almost seven years before I made the transition to an organization that required emergency shelters to be set up in Hope, British Columbia. In 2019, God moved me into a new position where I would learn the skills that I required to fulfill the plans and purposes He had for my life. As Program Manager, Residential Programs and Shelter," my experience was expanded over the next year. My time in this position was cut short as I was limited in my opportunities to use the name of "Jesus" or refer to "God" as a source of healing.

I spent the next year completing my studies at "Rhema" Bible School and received my Graduate Diploma in 2020. With my newfound knowledge of God's word, Holy Spirit prompted me to set up homes for Children in Care. In 2021 I took a leap of faith where I spent my last $1000 of available credit on my credit card to set up "Touching Hearts Family Services Inc." God honored my step of faith, and the day after I did this, I was awarded my first contract and was able to open what is now known as "Allison House." As the reputation of our quality of service became known, it was not long before I had four homes running. I still find it a little overwhelming when I consider where I came from to where I am now, as President and CEO of a multi-million-dollar company with over 40 employees. The exciting thing is that God is not finished yet, as He has birthed a Vision within me to provide facilities for individuals suffering from PTSD and for mothers and their children who are in treatment for addictions. As of October 2022, I brought my husband on staff to design and prepare the layout drawings for these facilities. God had this all planned. Just as He took my life experiences, He took Bob's Engineering experience and brought us together to fulfill His plan. **Our God is truly Awesome.**

Special Invitation

Now that you have read my life story in great detail, you know how my personal relationship with Jesus has transformed my life. I was damaged, I was broken, I was lost, and I had no hope, yet He received me as His own at the very instant I recognized His sovereignty. Jesus redeemed me from the pit of hell by giving His life for mine on the cross at Calvary. With His life, with His shed blood, He paid the price for my sin. After He saved me, He then filled me with His Holy Spirit so that I could walk in the power and in the authority that He wants every believer to have.

Would you like to have what I have? Do you want to receive God's offer of eternal life and hope? If you do, the process is quite simple. Just pray the following prayer and mean it from your heart.

Dear God, I know and believe that Jesus is your Son and that He died on the cross and was raised from the dead. Because I am a sinner and need forgiveness, I ask Jesus to come into my heart. I am willing to change the direction of my life by acknowledging Jesus as my Lord and Saviour and by turning away from my sins. Thank you for giving me forgiveness, eternal life, and hope.

In Jesus' Holy Name,

Amen.

If you have prayed this prayer, let me welcome you into the family of God. Now that you have made the decision to come into a personal relationship with Jesus, there are some things I would encourage you to do.

- Be open to receiving the Holy Spirit just as the converts did in the book of Acts. Ask and receive the Spirit just as you received salvation.

- If you are presently not attending a church, find yourself a church that teaches the gospel message of hope to all who accept Christ as their Lord and Saviour, which is the only way we can receive forgiveness, purpose, and eternal life.

- Study God's word because that's where you'll find the true answers to all the questions you have.

- Allow Holy Spirit to minister to you and teach you how to listen for His still, small voice.

- Be water baptized, by immersion, just as Jesus said you should be.

As you now begin a new chapter in your Journey, please remember that you are no longer traveling alone because Jesus is with you. In what is known as the "Great Commission," Jesus Himself speaks these words,

Matthew 28:20 (NIV)

20: . . . "And surely I am with you always, to the very end of the age."

May God bless you and watch over you as you begin or continue on your Journey.

Sharon Holburn

Epilogue

When I first became involved in ministry to women who had been used and abused, I quickly realized that my life experiences enabled me to say to these women, "I've been where you're at. I know how you feel because I have felt the hurt and pain that you are feeling." While it was a rewarding experience for me to be able to help these women, it was also frustrating for me as I was limited to a one-on-one situation. In preparing this book, my initial focus was to get my story into a medium that would give me greater exposure to many who need to read my story. As I have worked through the preparation of this book, I have been given the opportunity to go back to the beginning and to relive and reevaluate many of my life experiences; the good, the bad, and the ugly. It may be hard for you to understand that this has been most beneficial for me because it has given me the opportunity to forgive those who have hurt me. Even though I can't say that I fully understand all things, I can honestly say that I now have a greater perception of the big picture, of God's big picture.

In searching out the many root causes of the issues in my life, I always seem to find myself back at the beginning, back when it was just my mother and me. Even though, in later years, my mother received salvation, she never did receive the healing that was available for her because she chose to remain a very broken and hurting woman. In spite of how she had treated me, my only prayer for her was that she would choose to receive the healing that God so desperately wanted to give to her. She only had to ask, and it would have been given. She only had to receive, and it would have been hers, a healing that would have covered all the hurt and the brokenness in her life. Regretfully she chose not to ask or to receive, and the result was that she lived her life as a broken, hurting individual, never really experiencing life to the fullest.

As you have read this book, you have seen that there were many times in my life when it really hurt to be me. Yet, even though my life has been difficult and painful at times, I can thank God for the opportunity of experiencing my life as I have lived it. What has made it so worthwhile is that I have been able to show people that, in spite of what their life experiences have been, joy and freedom can come through Jesus Christ. I have seen firsthand the freedom that sharing my story has brought to so many and the glory it has brought to God. Just as a former alcoholic can minister more effectively to an individual who is addicted to alcohol, through my life experiences, I am fully equipped to minister healing and deliverance to the broken and hurting people of the nations. My Abba Father took everything in my life that was meant for evil and has used it for good, bringing untold glory to His name because it never really was about me. It was always all about Him. Now that you have read all about my Journey and my pathway to freedom, I offer this prayer to God on your behalf.

Father, I pray that as your children walk through their paths of life that they will reach out and take hold of your hand.

Father, I pray that they will learn to trust you, just as I have learned to trust you.

Father, I pray that you will break off the chains of bondage that hold your children captive.

Father, I further pray that you will supernaturally deliver them from the hand of the enemy and that the destiny you have spoken into their lives will come to pass.

Father, I take authority over the enemy, and I push back in the spirit realm every demonic force that would try to destroy the lives of your people.

Father, I bind every tactic of the enemy, and I cancel the assignments that the enemy has placed on their lives, rendering them all useless in the name of Jesus.

Father, I pray that your mighty hand of protection will be upon your people.

Father, I pray that you will give them eyes to see and ears to hear what you have to say. I decree and declare that every person whose hand touches this book would be set free in Jesus' Holy name.

Amen.

Mission Statement

Isaiah 61:1

1: The Spirit of the Sovereign Lord is on me, because the Lord has anointed me to proclaim good news to the poor. He has sent me to bind up the brokenhearted, to proclaim freedom to the captives and release from darkness the prisoners,

Manufactured by Amazon.ca
Acheson, AB

11481109R00162